KEY WEST COLLECTION

KEY WEST COLLECTION

DOROTHY RAYMER

Photographs by Tom Corcoran

THE KETCH & YAWL PRESS

~ KEY WEST, FLORIDA ~

Front Cover Photograph © 1978 Tom Corcoran
Inside Photographs © Tom Corcoran
All Photo Rights Reserved
Book Design by Tom Corcoran

Published by The Ketch & Yawl Press
              PO Box 6891, Lakeland FL 33807
                    and
              Key West Island Book Store
              531 Fleming Street, Key West FL 33040
              (888) 715-0723 / e-mail: kwbook@aol

International Standard Book Number: 0-9641735-4-9

Printed in the United States of America

DEDICATION
AND
ACKNOWLEDGEMENTS

Key West Collection is dedicated to William (Bill) Huckel, former publisher and editor of *Solares Hill*. Bill rescued me from the fatal ennui of retirement in 1977, and gave me an outlet for further writing, as well as granting me assignment copyright for the stories which first appeared in *Solares Hill* and are now in this book.

Acknowledgements are in varying degrees, and for numerous reasons, to scores of people. I can't list all of them since there are so many. I can only express my gratitude in general, and list some of the very special contributors who were generous with technical assistance, or information; with advice, encouragement, time and effort in numerous capacities. And above all, who sustained me with faith and encouragement. I ask for forgiveness in advance for inadvertent omission of individual credit in helping to produce this book.

Back in 1962, Lt. Cmdr. Edward Raymer (suspected but no proven relationship) and his wife, Marilyn Raymer, who were stationed in Key West with the U.S. Navy, helped me through a rough financial crisis and kept urging me to keep writing the material for a book. To them, first bow. After that comes the accolade to Richard Marsh, editor, and Terry Risko and Norma Maccubbin, then of the Key West Island Bookstore, for the venture into publishing.

Deep-hearted thank you is due Lynne Armantrout for her aid in correspondence and in getting proper copies made of book segments. Jim Tucci, of the *Key West Citizen*, deserves special attention for his accurate typing and rush work, gratis, plus wise advice.

All of the Monroe County Library staff were cooperative in the research I did. Gold stars go to Sylvia Knight for her extraordinary "detective" method in tracing material; to Betty Bruce, Donna Marsh and Julie Williams, plus Rhoni Goldstein, for patience and persistence in research for me. Jay Garon, literary agent, deserves applause for his original guidance. Valuable help in research of records provided by Alvin Smith and all the members of the Monroe County Courthouse crew in charge of official files can take bows for assistance.

Wayne Pelke, Resident Center Director, St. Leo's College, Naval Air

Station, Key West, edited the Van Cosel yarn, cutting it to acceptable size. Wright Langley arranged a taped interview with "Red" Beccaise for "The Bad Old Days" chapter, and helped me in other ways. Jo Ann Savio is responsible for the photographs taken during my Tennessee Williams interview. Tennessee, himself, proffered excellent advice as well as expressed confidence in my endeavor. Additional personal acknowledgements are included in the actual sequences of *Key West Collection*.

Tangible and intangible credits are due a number of other people, friends and well-wishers. Among them, I single out Eleanor Walsh, Joan and Edward Knight, Norman Artman, and Capt. Tony Tarracino. Cmdr. and Mrs. Lee Goddard, Capt. and Mrs. Frank Bowser, Margaret Foresman, Lola Curry, Erasto Perez, Alyce Milan, Frank Carpentier, Tim Miller, Don Pinder, Joe Pinder, Florence Spottswood, Chino Fraga, Cmdr. Herbert Whitney, Charlie Ramos, Florence Fuller, Gloria Bollens, Sebastian Cabrera Ill, Janice White, Ann Carleton, Louis Carbonell, Poly Artman, Louise and David Wolkowsky, who so generously loaned the painting by Tennessee Williams for the original edition's front cover.

The list is practically unlimited, and so I stop now, but with a final tribute to all of those who helped in diverse ways.

-Dorothy Raymer

THE AUTHOR

Dorothy Raymer was a fixture of Key West journalism from 1949 until her death in June 1982. She was a columnist and feature writer for the *Key West Citizen* and *Solares Hill*, sketching past and present island scenes and characters.

Her writing credits included book and entertainment columns for the *Miami News* and brief stints with other publications, as well as assignments for high school and college papers and short stories and poems for her fourth grade teacher. She received her Master's in English Literature from Ohio State University in 1931, after being "requested to withdraw" from Thiel College in Pennsylvania for writing a paper for a sociology course entitled "Woman Is Not an Incubator." She also had a postscript graduate year at Antioch College. She lived for years in a Conch house that was built in 1886 on a short, narrow lane originally called "Gruntbone Alley," from the residents' habit of throwing fish bones into the street.

Loved, respected, pampered, and spoiled by her many fans and friends on the island, and a genuine character herself, Dorothy was the subject of a large collection of "no-one-but-Dorothy" lore that rivaled her own "Only in Key West" vignettes for pure outrageousness. She was immortalized in literature by two authors:

The hero's lover in David Loovis's Key West novel, *The Last of the Southern Winds,* was given Dorothy's physical description, mannerisms, and job at the local paper. In Tennessee Williams's play *The Gnagdiges Fraulein* (included in his book Dragon Country), she showed up as Polly, the "southernmost gossip columnist and Society Editor of the southernmost news organ in the Disunited Mistakes" —a rollicking comedy role.

FOREWORD

Key West Collection was originally published in 1981 by the Key West Island Book Store. When John Boisonault purchased the store in 1986, the rights to the book came along with the deal. As we go to press, in mid-1999, the book has been out of print, unavailable for almost six years. On the urging of Wright Langley, our local book distributor, author, and historian, we decided to reissue *Key West Collection.*

Dorothy Douthitt Raymer was the perfect blend of transplanted northerner and converted islander. An independent woman, she feared little. Her faithful canine companion, Geronimo, feared even less. Key West residents lived in terror of having Dorothy reveal old secrets and legends; at the same time they couldn't wait to bend her ear. They knew how effectively she retold the old tales, how she had mastered the art of "just-between-you-and-me." Dorothy captured the feel of Key West, the personality that makes it more than just a beautiful, remote tropical outpost. As we read these stories today, they are not dated. Each seems to have happened just last week, or last year. Dorothy Raymer understood the free spirit that helped create today's Key West, and much of it exists on these pages.

In researching Dorothy's original articles, we found text that was omitted from the original book; when possible, that text has been added. While we consulted with several individuals mentioned in the book (or who lived in Key West during the period Dorothy described), we received only confirmation of name spellings and business locations. We have edited for format consistency, and deleted little. We did not change text to re-write Dorothy's take on history. It was her newspaper column; it remains her book.

-John Boisonault
-Tom Corcoran

TABLE OF CONTENTS

KEY WEST COLLECTION

THE BAD OLD DAYS

The word "establishment" had a different meaning in the early days of Key West than it has now. Instead of the usual connotation, meaning a group of conservative persons in government, civic or business groups, around the turn of the century "establishment" was a word commonly associated with a house of ill-repute, an establishment of prostitution. The city was peppered with dozens of establishments, most of them in conjunction with a bar and dance floor. Several were connected with gambling places.

One of the most popular of the bawdy houses was known as Alice Reid's, located at 1016 Howe Street. It was a two-story structure with a modest yard planted in crotons, hibiscus and other native plants and vines. A traditional red light near the front door designated the type of business on the premises.

Upon entering the main room downstairs, visitors faced a large bar at the rear of the room. There was a jukebox on the right, a piano, and a compact dance floor surrounded by little tables, chairs and a lounge or two. Nothing truly grandiose or elegant, as the Silver Dome on 54th Street in Miami, or Old World, as the bordellos in Havana, Cuba. But Alice Reid's house was fairly presentable and cleanly kept.

Alice Reid's was noted for a brand of southern hospitality as soothing as Southern Comfort, which was one of the most called-for drinks at that time. During prohibition, there was no lack of rum, either, for Key West was the port of rum runners operating out of Cuba and the Bahamas.

According to a well-informed Key Wester, the trains of the Flagler Railroad Extension, coming from the mainland loaded with tourists and not-so-tired businessmen, were greeted at the Florida East Coast Terminal here by a fleet of taxis, all Model T and Model A Fords. The passengers were openly solicited by cab drivers to sample the wares of different whorehouses.

Alice Reid's on Howe Street drew a large share of the fleshpot trade, but there were other places in the pre-World War II era which were well-patronized by locals. Among them was The Square Roof, in the neighborhood of Reid's, but at Petronia and Emma Streets in what was called Jungle Town. The customers being catered to were white; the girls varied in skin tones from light to dark. A smaller house was Florine's, located where Douglass School now is.

Big Annie's was another site of relaxation and amusement. There is conflicting opinion of its location. Some say it was just off Duval Street on a backway path called Cherry Lane, bisecting a trailer park tract where the *Key West Citizen* parking lot is at present.

Noteworthy information is that Big Annie reportedly used the love-for-sale enterprise proceeds to put her daughter through college. Whereby the daughter turned away from academic pursuits and followed in her mother's boudoir slipper steps, establishing a profitable house of her own near the original Big Annie's, and adding a gambling concern to the prostitution efforts.

The smallest place of dalliance known to the public was The Yellow House, or just "The 100," a home at the end of Truman Avenue, handy to the Naval Station. There were only two or three women on duty there.

Most houses were occupied by six to ten prostitutes. Early on, the going rate for services was only two dollars. This increased to a three dollar average, and, as demand increased, so did the fees, until five dollars was considered the adequate sum per session.

The girls themselves were required to pay a percentage to the madam or proprietor of the house. For that reason, there were quite a few prostitutes operating from their own homes, and they were scattered all over the town. Most of the "independents" had their own "pimps," who drove their own cars as taxis and took a rakeoff from the business they drummed up for the individual girls.

The well-known Mom's, which moved to Stock Island, was originally located in Old Town, at Amelia and Thomas Streets. The day that Mom's stable moved to Stock Island and became known as Mom's Tea Room was described in an article by Jose Yglesia of Miami, whose grandfather was born in Key West.

Yglesia wrote his article for *Venture* magazine, and it appeared in February 1969, entitled, "Key West: of Sailors, Shrimps and The Way It Was." Written with dash, set in a bold frame, the story stated that the waterfront stretch on Front Street, along three blocks to Mallory Square, was once "all gambling or bawdy houses."

As Yglesia tells it, the move of the houses of ill repute to the hinterland was begun shortly after the end of World War II. It was perhaps several years earlier for Mom's trek to Stock Island, where she installed her girls in a large two-story bungalow on MacDonald Avenue. Palm trees clustered around the entire property, sheltering the house somewhat, and there was a degree of seclusion.

However, the downstairs had a spacious verandah which faced

MacDonald Avenue, and the inmates of the "tea room" often waved to passing cars and bicyclists while they sat sunning themselves on the porch.

Artist Karl Agricola used to laugh about the cheery greetings exchanged daily with Mom's girls as he wheeled by on his bike en route to his home and studio out on what is called "The Point."

Mom's move to Stock Island was a gala event, with fanfare. Mom rode in a lead car and announced her new address over a loud-speaker and invited everybody to visit the new premises. The motorcade traveled down Duval Street with the girls riding grandly, two in each vehicle, twirling parasols and bowing and waving left and right to watchers along the way. One report had it that a ukulele band strummed jazz tunes as the cars rolled by.

The vanishing of "controlled" prostitution was lamented by many outspoken citizens. They waxed indignant over the loss of available females in a Navy town. "When you have a lot of young bucks all together in one small place, whores are a necessity. As it is, the sailors will run after our good girls, and women residents won't be safe on the streets," railed one complaining Conch.

Alice Reid's place was perhaps the best known of the houses in the city limits, not only because of the verbal advertising spread by the cab drivers, but for its actual enticements. The girls were nearly all from Georgia, had "honey-chile" accents and were nearly all wholesome, country-style, nice-looking "fillies." Exuding Southern charm, they were appealing, for the most part, not overly exotic, and they made customers feel truly welcomed. All the Reid girls were dressed in virginal white! Such quality of allure and innocence provided a winsome combination.

As an old-timer on the island related it, a successful and well-known member of the community married a woman who had worked in one of the "establishments," and she turned out to be a loyal and respectable helpmate. "She made a very good Conch wife," said the man-in-the-know.

The popularity of the Reid house was partly due to the discipline with which the operation was governed. The proprietors were Alice Reid and Marvin Griffith, reportedly a married couple. Rules were strictly kept, and the house closed its bar and bed business promptly at 2 A.M. The owner supervised the shuttering and kept order. All was well and the routine adhered to, except for one person.

This was a taxi driver who had the ironically Rabelaisian name of Plowman. Graydon Plowman was a secret visitor to Cecelia Thompson Tunks, one of the Georgia "honey-buns" who worked for Alice and Marvin. She was a large woman, about six feet tall. Some reports picture her as a redhead, others as having raven locks. But as one informant declared, "Those girls dyed their hair and made frequent changes in coloring, so who is to name the true color?"

It was a nightly custom for Plowman to keep a 3 A.M. rendezvous with Cecelia, meeting her in her own room a full hour after the Reid house was officially shuttered. Whether this was for romantic reasons or business arrangements is unknown. It could be that Plowman was simply checking up on receipts of trade he steered toward Cecelia, or he may have been enamored of her.

At any rate, Plowman kept his usual waltz-time appointment, so called from an old popular song, "Three O'Clock in the Morning." He climbed the outside back stairs that led to a second floor door to reach the room occupied by Cecelia Tunks. There was no answer to his knock, so he went around the second story porch where a window looked into her bedroom. He could see her in bed, so he climbed in the window and found her nude body sprawled on the top of the bedding.

The news report, with peculiar delicacy, stated she had been strangled "with a silken undergarment, twisted around her throat with a toothbrush."

Identification of the "undergarment" was never revealed in the news account, but it was later generally asserted that a pair of silk panties was used to accomplish the strangling.

The inquest, held February 11, was a confusing procedure with conflicting testimony by nearly all persons involved in any manner. Justice of the Peace Enrique Esquinaldo, who later became Municipal Judge, was hard put to get and coordinate accurate statements from witnesses.

Plowman's behavior following his discovery of the crime was odd. At the inquest he told questioner J. Lancelot Lester, Jr., that after seeing that Cecelia was dead, he rushed out via the window and the back stairs in shock, without rousing anyone in the house. He then walked, still in shock, seven blocks to a downtown bar, where he finally took a taxi to inform the police of the death.

Bartender Chester Roberts, employed by the Griffiths, testified that he had last seen the victim at around 11:30 P.M. in the downstairs area, but not after that time.

A close girlfriend of Cecelia's reported that she had noticed her in the bar at 12:40 A.M. The other six "on the staff" couldn't recall just when the big redhead had appeared in the bar section. They all

6

explained that they were required to be in the contact space at the bar unless they were in their respective rooms dealing with clients.

One girl remarked that she had heard a noise around 2 A.M., as if a heavy person had dropped from the low roof outside the window of her room.

Dr. H. C. Galey examined the corpse and told of bruises found on the deceased women's face, one on her chin and another under one eye. The physician placed the time of the murder at approximately ten hours before he had examined the strangled woman–which pointed to about 2 A.M., February 9 as the hour the crime was committed.

A special investigator from the State Attorney's office in Miami arrived to grill all persons involved with the event. He was assisted in fingerprinting by Roy Hamlin.

Auburn Ellis, a steward on a yacht docked here, was one of the men interrogated. He admitted that he had gone with Cecelia to her room, but then returned to the bar and was seen there before he returned to his ship.

It was learned that the murdered woman was only twenty-two years of age, and that she came originally from Roseville, Georgia. She had lived in Key West for about three years. In October 1940, she had married a Navy man who served aboard the USS *Pandora*, which was presently out of the country.

Mr. and Mrs Marvin Griffith (she was better known as Alice Reid) were held as material witnesses, as was bartender Chester Roberts, but after a number of weeks the case was still unsolved and the witnesses were released. There were rumors that the strangling was an "inside job," and that one of the house prostitutes, or Alice Reid herself, had been the strangler. The motive, according to scuttlebutt, was that Marvin Griffith had been getting overly "chummy" with Cecelia Tunks. Opinions varied, especially since Cecelia had been a large woman capable of defending herself, particularly if another woman had been her attacker. There was also a hint that a Lesbian element may have been the cause behind the homicide.

During the six weeks of investigation, the Reid house was temporarily out of action, and, due to several raids, it missed participation in a convention of one of the largest men's organizations in the country. This loss of revenue, plus persistent interference by the FBI, who stepped into the community and arrested seven women for vagrancy, was the coup de grace. After a couple of repeats in this line, the Alice Reid house ceased operations, and so did the other bawdy houses.

In addition to the FBI charges of white slavery brought against operators of brothels on the island, the U.S. Navy demanded a general cleanup of houses of prostitution. With the approach of the nation's participation in World War II, the campaign against whorehouses continued, and concentrated action against prostitution resulted in abandonment of Key West's organized red-light habitats. Of course there continued to be scattered "services" available, including "business as usual" by independent streetwalkers and "B-girls" about town. But the days of fame of the houses of ill-fame were over.

THE SPELL WAS CAST

When I first told colleagues in Miami that I was planning to move to Key West, it was the spring of 1948. They all seemed aghast that I was going to leave the "safety of the mainland" and the bright lights of show business and civilization for an isolated island, a "jumping off place" at the end of Florida. Now it is a "jumping on" place. Dire predictions were made of what would happen to me in a place so tough that even the worms that attacked the bottoms of boats ate right through copper layers which were supposed to protect their hulls.

The natives were described as descendants of pirates and wreckers who lured ships onto the reefs with placement of false lights. And, according to my informers, the natives were restless. If Conchs didn't like you, you were ambushed and bopped on the head, and perhaps they might set fire to your abode. Maybe you would simply be driven to the line between Monroe County, where Key West is located, and Dade County, then abandoned. Or taken up the Keys in a boat and dropped overboard in mosquito-ridden mangrove swamps where alligators could be heard grunting in the dark.

Eyebrows were elevated when I expressed my desire to move to Key West, despite all the foreboding. "You want to live in that outpost hamlet? They had Ernest Hemingway there for years, but he finally took off for Cuba. And baby, *he* was *rugged!*"

"President Truman likes it there," I countered.

The answer: "But he has a Secret Service bodyguard and he stays on the Naval Station at the Little White House, surrounded by protective Naval security. A lone woman can't even come home from the movies without being accosted by sex-mad sailors, or arrested for street-walking by police who don't speak English."

"You'll end up being a 'wreck ashore,'" I was forewarned.

However, I was willing to take my chances. After all, I had been staying in Key West off and on for some time. I had painted word pictures of serene evenings when the soft violet and lilac hours descended on the lush tropical setting, and enchanting chimes of a church sounded at sunset, an old custom from the past.

"You evidently don't know *why* the bells ring around sundown," one newsman told me. "Lemme tell you. It's an old tradition, okay, a hangover from the years when the bells clanged out the hour for

9

hanging pirates."

But I had long ago succumbed to the lure of Key West and was impervious to all the advice to "beware." I was determined to abandon the turmoil and strain of a world I had known as movie and nightclub editor on the *Miami Daily News* for more than four years.

As a matter of true record, once upon a diary, I had written an entry as far back as 1941 on sensing the sorcery of Casa Cayo Hueso.

I wrote about my first visit to Key West, made January 1, 1941. I still have that New Year's entry to prove that I was entranced in just one brief afternoon tour of the island. The spellbinding began on that initial drive and became a decisive turning point in my life eight years later. The journey from Miami to Key West over the newly opened Overseas Highway, some forty years ago, was one of the lures in itself. I remember making the drive with friends in a venerable Ford coupe with a rumble seat. I was ensconced in "the rumble" and reveled in the sweep of salt-scented wind, the high, blue vault of a cloudless sky, and a vivid sense of freedom, away from the tumultuous city of Miami. There was little traffic, and the borders of the highway were much less cluttered with signs.

The bridges along the route beckoned from key to key, permitting side glimpses of expanses of water, silken stretches in jewel tones of pale sapphire, tourmaline, lapis lazuli, and turquoise, with now and then a layer of deep amethyst where seaweed tinted the surface.

We reached Key West in mid-afternoon and drove around what is now known as Old Town and the narrow lanes and broader avenues, admiring the unique architecture, the widow's walks, the gingerbread on old buildings. I loved the big mahogany shade trees, the patios and gardens seen briefly through iron fences and gates in walls, the peaked silvery roofs, gabled windows, spacious, stately homes, and subtle quality of Old World atmosphere.

As we left the city, I was especially impressed with a tall, weather-beaten wooden house, framed in arching trees, the front facade mysterious-looking, with a second story verandah, also unpainted, retaining the patina of time. I learned in subsequent investigation that this was the old Kemp home, corner of Caroline and Simonton Streets. Each time I pass it I recall looking up at the house from the confines of the car and resolving to return someday to explore the premises.

Came World War II in December of that fateful 1941. So many years passed before I could fulfill the self-made promise to come back. In the interim, between then and 1949, when I moved here permanently, I managed to visit the isle of enchantment on numerous occasions. Each visit established a closer rapport with the community I had come to know and love.

I was still writing a column for the *Miami Daily News* amusement pages, of which I was editor, when I got an invitation to see a special performance of the great dancer, Ted Shawn. He and his partner, Ruth St. Denis, had been favorites of mine ever since I had seen them dance in Pittsburgh when I was in my early teens.

This time, Shawn was appearing solo as guest star in a dance recital to be presented by Paul Baron, resident of Key West, who had often been on Miami Beach nightclub tours.

One of his repeat show business deals was at the Kitty Davis Airliner, a Beach bistro popular all during World War II and the late 1940s, so we were well acquainted. I accepted the invitation with delight, and thereby swings the tale of my firm resolve to become a part of the Key West picture.

I was met at the airport by Baron and his partner, Norval Reed, who operated the Southernmost Flowers and Gift Shop. Reed was Baron's manager for nightclub dance performance engagements. They hired an open convertible, presented me with a lei of real gardenias, and even had a photographer on deck to take photos.

I was made to feel like a hotshot celebrity, and I adored the attention from the other side. In my career I was always viewing and interviewing celebrities, but had never had the experience of being treated as one myself. It's false glamour, but it was pleasant!

We drove through the late afternoon sunlight to the La Concha Hotel, which was near the shop/living quarters for Baron and Reed. I suppose my hosts had pre-arranged the next experience, but it was a complete surprise for me.

I was wearing an orange 'frou-frou' feathered hat, a chapeau which was chic at the time. (I understand such headgear is on the way back.) We drew up with a flourish at the La Concha's Duval Street entrance, and I stepped out on the sidewalk while a bellhop assembled my luggage, the procedure supervised by my gallant hosts.

Suddenly, from behind a pillar of the La Concha's colonnade, a startling figure popped up. I learned after the episode that the man was known as Coocoo Bobo, a character about town often hired for welcoming parties. He stared at my orange-feathered hat, and I stared at his plumed, fore-and-aft admiral's hat, vintage of the late 1890's. Besides the odd headgear, Coocoo Bobo wore an army tunic with outside épaulettes of shining braid and fringe. Across his chest was a triple row of decorations created from tin can tops and Gold Medal Flour medals.

Around his waist was a purple fringed sash, which was lettered in gold, "In fond memory of ——." The rest of the words disappeared in a jaunty bow tied over one hip, but undoubtedly it was adapted from a funeral wreath banner.

His baggy trousers seemed to be relics from cavalry riding days on the Mexican border, around the year 1915. They were khaki but bleached almost white, and were tucked into leather puttees of the World War I period. The puttees encased his sturdy but very bowed legs. And his feet, large and splayed, were completely bare.

Under one arm, Coocoo Bobo carried a sort of baton-flute, made of chrome casings. He put this to his lips and tootled out a series of blatant notes which had no tune, but were delivered with aplomb. Then he set aside the home-made instrument, bowed deeply from the waist, swept off the plumed hat and intoned, "The Ambassador of Key West welcomes you!"

Almost helpless with constrained laughter, I forced myself to start toward the hotel entrance. But Coocoo Bobo held up a halting hand like a traffic cop. He bowed again and said, "You must see choo-choo dance." Then, whistling and shuffling, he gave an exact imitation of a locomotive sounding a whistle while coming into a station under full steam, huffing and puffing, making his unshod feet sound the cadence of an engine approaching a station, then coming to the "chuh-chuh" stop. My hosts rewarded him with money and Coocoo Bobo made another hat-doffing salute before he wandered off.

"That does it!" I exclaimed. "This town is for me!"

After dinner that evening there was more excitement and funny experiences which added to the enticement Key West held for me.

The dance recital was held at the Senior High School, now the Glynn Archer Elementary School at White and United Streets. The murals at either side of the auditorium stage attracted my attention and admiration. They were painted by Bill Hoffman during WPA days.

The dancing by Baron was vivid and Latin, with rhumba, a cape dance and other brilliant footwork numbers. Then Ted Shawn presented some of his classic routines, much appreciated by those who recognized artistry, even though he was by then an aging star.

The dance which won the most applause, and certainly my plaudits for his adjustable approach (which turned from a near disaster into a personal triumph), centered on an adaptation from a sacred dance of the Isle of Crete. Shawn surged out on stage in a tunic-like costume and crested helmet. He began a strange maneuver, lifting his legs high and stomping in a slow, patterned dance. In each clenched hand he held a small battle mace. He would pause in pompous strut and shake first one mace and then the other. It was in a way ludicrous, but nobody laughed. Instead there was a surprising reaction. The first three or four rows in the auditorium were packed with youngsters. At first they were transfixed by Ted Shawn's ritual parading and stomping and were silent. But when he stepped to the footlights and shook one mace and then the other in obvious defiance, the children aped the gestures, fists raised on high.

Instead of being angered, Shawn broke into a grin. He and the children exchanged roars of challenge and more warlike gestures. The kids were fascinated, and not only clapped loudly but shouted in delight, not derision. Shawn was cheered at the conclusion of his performance, and the entire audience gave him a standing ovation.

In an interview after the recital, Shawn remarked, "It's great to be appreciated and understood by the younger generation. This island has true joie de vivre and lots of character."

It still has.

A robust laugh finale to the evening's entertainment was unwittingly provided by me. I had an aisle seat on the right hand side of the crowded auditorium, about a dozen rows from the front. It was cordoned off with tape and a sign. At intermission I rose with the rest of the audience and walked slowly up the aisle toward the exit.

I first became aware that something was amiss by snickers and giggling behind me, then subdued laughter ahead of me as people passed me. But it was not until I had made my way into the lobby that I discovered the source of the polite but persistent amusement.

A very dignified usher reached behind me, made a quick grab at my dress at the lower part of my back and held up the taped sign that had marked my place. It had somehow become attached to my rump. He murmured with a wink, "Perhaps you would like this for a souvenir?" and handed over the sign.

Advice is given to always read the bottom line.

My bottom line read: "RESERVED FOR THE PRESS."

JUST WILD ABOUT HARRY

I was a "stringer" for North American Newspaper Alliance back in 1948-49 when I got my first glimpse of President Truman. He had already begun to visit Key West periodically on his work-vacations at The Little White House on the Key West Naval Station, part of the big base here.

It was October 1948, with election month looming in the near future. The story I submitted on Truman's visit was not published by NANA because it arrived too late. But the story still serves as one of the zestier episodes, and was one of the reasons why I decided that I was going to move to Key West permanently.

The presidential entourage first visited Miami. President Truman would address American Legion convention delegates at Dinner Key, then return to the old airport on Northwest 36th street for departure. The road to the airport was lined with sweating spectators who doffed coats and ties in late afternoon sunlight slanting in from the Everglades.

One watcher, a tobacco-chewing truck driver, yelled, "Y'awl must be expectin' Eugene Talmadge"–then the Governor of Georgia.

A huge garbage truck from the suburb of Miami Springs rolled to a stop at the junction of Le Jeune Road and 36th Street, right at the best vantage point for viewing the Presidential motorcade. The workers climbed out and stood atop the pile of garbage. The frantic traffic patrol had no sooner got the ill-smelling truck out of sniffing distance from the Truman motorcade, when a horse van, bringing race horses to Hialeah track, tried to back into position near a service station. People roared in anger, protesting the blocking of their view of the approaching Presidential party. The van driver finally gave up and drove on.

Finally, down the line came a Redtop Aerocar with a motorcycle escort, sirens screaming. Camera owners crawled on top of parked cars and shinnied up telephone poles and trees bordering the route. But it was a false alarm, not the arrival of President Truman and his family, but some other important passengers going to the airport. I never found out who they were, but they had a sense of humor. The four or five passengers looked out of the car windows and smilingly bowed to the confused throng.

The watchers were finally rewarded, and the real show rolled along the road, guarded by Miami's crack motorcycle police patrol, Secret Service squads, and other guards. Half a dozen limousines were in the lineup.

But the big moment was anti-climactic. The President was hatless, but his daughter, Miss Margaret Truman, made up for the lack. On her head was a spectacular creation of orchid felt with a wide brim swept high on one side and swooping to her shoulder on the other. It was crowned with a feather plume following the rakish lines of the chapeau–and it completely obscured her mother, Bess Truman, who sat by her side.

Street sweepers and the garbage truck crews stood at attention, lifting shovels, rakes and other work implements in salute to the President.

During that autumn I began visiting Key West more frequently, gradually preparing to make the island my permanent address. I made inroads, getting acquainted and cementing friendships with townspeople such as Jeanne Porter Kirke, daughter of the late Jessie Porter Newton, and Opal Van Deusen, who operated the Old Island Trading Post, corner of Caroline and Whitehead Streets. The shop was owned by "Miss Jessie," who was then Mrs. Kirke.

The chief salesgirl at the Old Island Trading Post was DeeDee Bessiere, a friend of Jeanne's and a lovely, tall, slender girl who looked like a high fashion model. One day she called me from Key West with a story she thought I would like for NANA, and she was correct.

Mrs. Truman was a rather shy woman who avoided social gatherings when she could. In Key West, her favorite "outing" was to come out the 1908 Presidential gate on Whitehead and cross over to the Old Island Trading Post, which is now part of the Pigeon House Patio Restaurant.

While her daughter, Margaret, shopped, Bess Truman liked to seat herself in a comfortable old rocking chair in the back room of the shop and chat with women friends who happened to be there, or with visitors, the wives of Washington VIPs who were here for conferences with the President. Secret Service men always accompanied Margaret and Bess Truman on their shopping tours, but the atmosphere was relaxed, and the Secret Service was pressed into additional services, carrying packages.

The long distance message from DeeDee revealed that Margaret Truman had been buying antique teacup and saucer sets, including miniatures, and that she was collecting them. The NANA story, circulated by syndicate, resulted in an "avalanche" of fancy teacups being sent to Miss Truman at the White House in Washington.

In fact, on the last sojourn in Key West, years later, when the doughty ex-President held a press conference in the La Concha Hotel during a visit with the late Senator John Spottswood, Bess Truman recalled the incident. When we were re-introduced, she paused and said, "Oh, I remember you! You were the reporter who wrote about my daughter's collection of teacups. We were absolutely swamped with presentations of them."

In November 1948, after Harry Truman had been re-elected to a full term, he came back on his fourth visit to his working-vacation hideaway. Key Westers shared in his triumph. They had voted for Truman ten to one, with only 500 local votes cast for Thomas Dewey at the island polls.

The mayor of Key West at that time was the late A. Maitland Adams, who issued a proclamation making Sunday, November 7, the date of the President's arrival in Key West, "Harry S. Truman Day." Some enterprising official suggested that the Chief Executive be presented, in a public ceremony, with a case of the savory green turtle soup canned by Thompson Enterprises, Inc., a firm in which the mayor had a business interest.

I interviewed Mayor Adams. He said, "That is out of the question. We want the President to enjoy our restful atmosphere and relax. We aren't intending to commercialize his visits. Lots of tourists come to see him, of course, but if President Truman keeps honoring us by coming here again and again, as he has, and as we hope he continues to do, needing a quiet rest, that's what we aim to give him."

People were permitted to greet the President if they saw him on the street. The First Baptist Church on Eaton Street arranged for Truman and his group to attend regular services. On his public appearances, the Key West High School Band was assigned to play. A small, select committee formed the official welcoming unit. The group was composed of the Mayor; John Spottswood, then a radio executive; Everett Russell; Judge William V. Albury; and local newsmen. Most of the fanfare was handled by the U.S. Navy.

That November 7, 1948, Key West citizens turned out in force, lining the route from Boca Chica Naval Air Base to the newly painted gate at the foot of Caroline, with cheers, enthusiastic applause, and shouts of "Give 'em hell, Harry."

No private invitations were thrust at Truman; such acts were considered a breach of etiquette. Still, Key Westers were deeply appreciative of the Presldent's attention to the city, and the consideration of renaming one of the island's main thoroughfares became a reality.

Division Street, an extension of Roosevelt Boulevard, was changed to Truman Avenue.

Brisk morning walks in streets adjacent to the U.S. Naval Station bounded by Whitehead once led the President to stop for a cup of coffee at The Caribe Restaurant, a glass and brick modern structure. It was located on Front Street, where Billie's Restaurant and Bar is now. The Caribe was owned by Sebastian Cabrera III. President Truman paid for his coffee with a dollar bill. Cabrera had the bill framed and hung on the wall of this establishment. He also enclosed the coffee cup and saucer in a glass case with the cup and saucer unwashed, as sort of shrine in memory of Truman. Later, somebody broke into the restaurant and stole the dollar bill, but Cabrera removed the encased cup and saucer and still has them, unwashed, at his home.

The devotion to Truman has remained unsullied in other ways. The poker table he had especially made has been preserved as a museum item. He and his card-playing cronies enjoyed many a game at The Little White House during his eleven stays here.

Merchants in town sent gifts to President Truman, and some were acceptable. I had a personal acknowledgement, in a White House letter, thanking me for a watercolor painted by the late Gerald Leake, which I had in my gift shop. It was a small, attractive view of the Little White House and was accepted as a souvenir. I also sent a lignum vitae walking stick made in the Virgin Islands, but I never found out if it was ever received. Nobody sent tributes for personal or commercial recognition.

By 1949, appearances in Key West by the President had become more and more frequent, and the populace never let down in their demonstration of affection for the Man from Missouri. One of the reasons for this was Harry Truman's showmanship. For example, in 1949, on one of the trips to Key West, he arrived on a Sunday afternoon from Washington and was greeted with a shower of confetti strands. During the processional ride from Boca Chica through the outskirts of Key West, then in the streets leading to the 1908 Presidential Gates, he let a strand of the paper ribbon cling to his sleeve as he rode in an open, sporty-looking cream-colored convertible. The green confetti fluttered in the sunshine.

Once inside the Naval Station gates, where formal reception ceremonies were to begin, Truman let the gala confetti spiral fall to the ground. There was an immediate stir among the spectators of Navy wives and children gathered just inside the entrance. If it hadn't been for the shoulder-to-shoulder barrier of sailors lined up in "manning the rail" formation, the souvenir hunters would have scrambled for the green streamer. One small urchin almost made it through the ranks, but was dragged back by his alert mother just before he could interrupt the traditional "piping aboard" ritual for the Commander-in-Chief.

In observance of the Sabbath, the usual 21-gun salute on this occasion was omitted. The Marine Guard of Honor and "Advance to the Colors" Ceremony made up for it. At this point, the Commanding Officer of the Marine Corps withdrew his sword and pointed it at a precise angle to the ground, ready to raise it in salute when the President emerged from his conveyance. A small dog evaded pursuit, darted up to the sword, and was about to give his own version of a salute with leg raised against the sword. The major in command flicked his sword broadside so that the flat steel edge deterred the dog. It ran off with a yip, and President Truman, observing what had happened, made a small moué, but restrained his humor and greeted the Marine CO with a straight face.

Despite the enthusiasm of the welcoming crowds, there was little lack of order. The only recorded loss of property occurred when the hero of the hour neared the terminal of the processional. Two small American flags had been placed in the upraised hand of the iron groomsman hitching post in front of the Old Island Trading Post. A fond mother removed one of the flags in order to stand her small child on the head of the postboy. The child, about three years old, promptly and with disregard of proper treatment of the American flag, seized the remaining flag and tossed it at Shore Patrolman standing by the curb.

After the police and Florida Road Patrol had cleared the streets of pedestrians, people gathered in friendly groups, exchanging comments and bragging about having seen "The Fighting Man of Washington." Amateur photographers compared notes on their field day ventures. Some of the pictures must have been startling, for a large number of Blacks turned out in home-sewn, sequined costumes topped with bizarre, spectacularly designed headgear for this special event. It was like a bit of Mardi Gras. The manager of the City Electric System, Charles A. Van Deusen, remarked, "Truman certainly looked confident, and that makes me feel much better about the future of the whole nation." After sundown, the bells of St. Paul's Episcopal Church chimed out "America." As the sound of the anthem died away, people paused in the streets of the city. Some bowed their heads, some looked up at the sky, and all were smiling.

The episodes in Key West connected with Truman in his heyday weren't always reverent, but they were never a tarnishing element. Rather, many of the happenings tended to humanize the Presidency and to bring Truman closer to his public. For example, in an early period, Truman tended to wear somewhat wild sport shirts in Key West, even when conducting press conferences. Then a couple of years later, the entire contingent of national news service correspondents and the television crew showed up in sport shirts or T-shirts. Truman was no "Queen Victoria" advocate and, as a general rule, the international news and photographer group were pretty well governed, but the President was not amused. He resented this display. The next session with the world-wide press representatives was toned down, with Truman himself setting a more sedate tone.

There was one incident when President Truman, presiding at a press conference on the lawn at the Little White House, was over-ruled–not because of rebellion, but because a photographer from a Latin American country did not understand English. When Truman called a halt to any more pictures, the Latin photographer ignored the order and kept right on snapping poses. He had to be forcibly removed from the scene.

A local nightclub, The Tradewinds, attracted the interest of the President, when he learned that singer Bob Ellis and Pianist Hal Prince had devised a special song. He sent a secret delegation to the club and obtained a recording of the entertainment. No official critique was released, but word got around that Truman enjoyed the presentation sung by Ellis and played by Prince.

In brief, the number opened with a song interlude asking, "Is it a bird? Is it a plane? Is it Superman? No! It's Truman!"

The opening lines were followed by a rousing section to the tune of a Sousa march: "Here come the boys of the press…," and a verse that advised, "Clean the streets up! Shine yo' shoes up…,"and on into a tune, with lyrics dedicated to the Truman regime.

Harry S. Truman was a foremost promoter of Key West through his eleven official working vacations here, and he continued to be a friend of the island in the years which followed his Presidency.

Presidents may come and they will certainly go, but Truman will remain deep in the memories of Key West forever.

JUSTIFIABLE HOMICIDE

For decades, a saying has been, "If you want to commit murder and get away with it, choose Key West." An early prime example was the recovery of a man's body in nearby waters. His feet were encased in a big tub of cement and his arms were secured behind him with binding wire. The coroner's jury verdict was suicide.

In the summer of 1949, I was new on the staff of the *Key West Citizen* and had never covered a crime story directly. I was assigned to the aftermath, the coroner's jury hearing, of what was known as "The Weaver Killing." This came about because the regular police beat reporter, Bill Lee, was incapacitated after spending most of his paycheck at Sloppy Joe's. He was back at his news desk when his irate spouse rode up upon her bicycle, stormed into the news room and felled her husband with a hefty clout administered with her parasol. Whether it was the blow on his head or the liquor or the combination, plus the shock of having "the little woman" at last rebel, Lee was hospitalized. I had to take over his beat.

The initial story was headlined, "Weaver Fatally Shot by Mrs. Weaver." Even as inexpert as I was in crime annals, I was startled at the lack of a more urgent headline. Nothing sensational, such as "Woman Shoots Estranged Mate" or "Wife Slays Ex-Husband." The following text read: "Thomas Albert Weaver, proprietor of a steak house at the foot of Duval Street, was fatally shot last night at 10:45 o'clock by his former wife as he sat in Weaver's Camp [a bar and restaurant] on Stock Island, which was being operated by his ex-wife. Weaver died in Monroe County Hospital a few minutes after his arrival."

David Newton, a *Miami Herald* reporter who'd been tipped about the shooting, drove immediately to the emergency ward. According to Newton, Weaver was bleeding profusely from multiple wounds. Newton exclaimed, "My God! He looks like a sieve. Is he dead?"

The examining doctor replied, "I haven't determined yet but, so far, I have found nine wounds." The ultimate count was eleven.

The shooting took place in the Weaver's Camp bar on the night of August 23. After the one-sided gunplay, Norvella Weaver sat and said calmly to the shocked audience of twenty-two witnesses, "Call the Sheriff." Deputy Sheriff Frank Webber responded and placed Mrs. Weaver under arrest. According to the news story, Mrs. Weaver said simply that she was "annoyed" by Weaver's trespassing on the property, and that she'd had a peace warrant issued to prohibit him from molesting her and their two children after a separation and divorce.

"Murder will out," and there was much more to the pumping of all those bullets into red-headed Weaver, who was known as a hot-tempered bully. I wrote the follow-through story for the August 25 *Citizen*:

A six-man coroner's jury convened in the office of the Justice of the Peace, the late Roy Hamlin, not far from the Monroe County Courthouse. The office was jammed to overflowing, and a throng of spectators lined the outside of the little building, climbing up on boxes, garbage cans, and chairs to peer in through windows. One enterprising man brought a little step-ladder and propped it up on the side of the building so that he looked into the room over my shoulder and breathed heavily down my neck.

Before the session got underway, the onlookers' exchanges of conversation were revealing. Among the comments:

"Tom Weaver was a red-headed summabitch, but he sure could turn out a good steak. Maybe she was jealous he was such a good cook, even though he only had that hole-in-the-wall at the corner of Duval and Front, and Norvella and her daddy run the Stock Island tavern."

"Listen, you dumdum! She killed him because, after they dee-vorced, he kept comm' around and threatenin' her. Wasn't no good for the restaurant business. She was a cool customer. After all them shots she just sat down and sez, 'Notify the Sheriff.' But somebody else say, 'Call the ambulance first,' because Tom wasn't dead yet. After them first shots, he fell on the floor and was moaning, 'Help me!' She seen he ain't dead yet. She got a second clip for her gun, straddled the body and swore, 'Now you're really gonna get it,' and fires five more shots."

"Nobody interfered? Not even after she reloaded?"

"Nope. Everybody was just paralyzed. Besides, when she was firing, a bullet ricocheted and hit a watcher in the leg. Nobody gonna brave all that shootin'."

There was more speculation. One comment was that "Mizz Weaver spent the whole afternoon practicing with her gun. She lined up beer cans on the fence behind the tavern. She said she was practicing on how to shoot rats."

Comment: "Well she got herself one! Weaver used to beat up on her all the time."

A young man sitting next to me on the left side of the J.P.'s office got my attention when he saw me taking notes. "Let me tell you the real motive behind this. Weaver came into the bar area and put forty-two nickels in the jukebox. It played the same record over and over again. I was there. I endured it and I loathed it. You want to know what that song was? It was called 'I Love You So Much It Hurts.' Well, no wonder she shot him!"

Justice of the Peace Roy Hamlin conducted the hearing with dignity. The defense attorneys were the late Julius Stone and Thomas Caro, who became Criminal Court Judge. And J. Lancelot Lester, Assistant State Attorney, conducted prosecution questioning.

The first witness to testify was Dr. Herman K. Moore, who had performed the autopsy. He was not the physician in residence at Monroe County General Hospital when Weaver was admitted. Moore proclaimed the Weaver had died from abdominal wounds which caused internal bleeding.

When asked how many bullets he had found in the body he replied, "There were eleven bullet holes, all told, but I didn't find any bullets."

Lester asked, "You mean all the bullets that penetrated had gone on through the body?"

Dr. Moore flashed dark eyes and answered, "I examined the wounds, yes, but I did not find any of the bullets, because the body was embalmed before I was called on to perform the autopsy."

After the hubbub which trailed his revelation had subsided, Coroner Hamlin dutifully pounded his gavel to quiet side remarks. He asked the "six wise men," as the jury was known, if there were any further questions.

"No questions, but we would like to hear Mrs. Weaver testify."

Lester leaped into the fray like a fighting bantam. He objected with the peppery statement that this session was "merely a hearing, not a trial."

Hamlin blandly asked the defense team how they felt about the matter. Tall, suave and every inch the Harvard lawyer, Julius Stone bowed to the coroner's jury and said, "My colleague and I would be delighted to have our client testify, if it would clear up circumstances in any way."

A jury vote and five minute recess was ordered. The "six wise men" made their way into a partitioned enclosure at the rear of the building. This was supposed to allow privacy and secrecy, but one of the men on the jury wore a hearing aid which was not functioning properly. As a result, the 'secret' conference was very loud, and listeners in the main room heard all the shouted comments to accommodate the hard-of-hearing juror. The foreman declared that he was very curious and would like to hear the details of Norvella Weaver's side of the episode.

Recess was announced by the Justice of the Peace while Mrs. Weaver was brought over from the County Courthouse jail where she was being held pending investigation. The mob dispersed to buy soft drinks and ice cream from vendors who had appeared and lent a carnival atmosphere to the hearing procedure.

Norvella Weaver, a willowy brunette, finally arrived, escorted by Deputy Frank Webber. She was dressed in somber black, save for a pair of twinkling rhinestone earrings. These were promptly removed on signal from her attorney, Julius Stone.

When she stood up to testify, she flashed her eyes toward the press section, then stood straight in front of the coroner's stand, twisting a plain white handkerchief in her hands. Otherwise, she maintained a controlled attitude. She had a thick "deep South" accent. She gave her age as twenty-seven, which surprised me, because she looked older. Of course this may have been due to complete lack of makeup, probably on lawyer's instructions.

She did not mention that she had become Tom Weaver's fourth or fifth wife after he had met her in Alabama, and that he had first been married to her sister, who had died under mysterious circumstances. Norvella did say, "I got lines in my face before my time because my husband made me take reducing pills. I was real heavy several years ago. And he shamed me in front of people and cussed me out. He even threatened to take my kids away, and he beat me sometimes."

At this point the icy surface calm was shattered and Norvella sobbed. "My two kids, they come to me and they ask real pitiful-like, 'Mama, how come Daddy don't love you no more?'" Norvella dabbed at her eyes with her handkerchief. The interlude brought clucks of sympathy from the crowd. I even saw one of the men in the jury box wiping his eyes with his tie.

As Norvella unraveled her harrowing life with her demanding and brutal spouse, and how she finally had divorced him, her accent became more Southern, but the tone remained determined. She told of having to swear out a warrant to keep herself safe and to stop Tom Weaver from disturbing the peace. "But he kept coming around the bar and saying terrible things about me to customers. So I went to the law again and swore out a trespassing bond against him," she said.

Infuriated, Weaver went to the home of a friend of Norvella, stuck a gun into the ribs of the woman, and forced her to telephone Norvella on the pretext of providing transportation from Stock Island to Key West.

Mrs. Weaver drove to her friend's home in a small truck, and when she stopped, Tom Weaver jumped out of a hiding place in the bushes. He pointed a gun at Norvella, she declared, and ordered her to drive back to the restaurant and demanded that she withdraw the trespassing restraint.

Incredible as it may seem, Norvella swore she struggled with her ex-husband even with the pistol confronting her. The gun went off, and he sustained a powder burn on his hand. In light of what happened afterward, this evidence stood Norvella in good stead.

In the ensuing confusion, she eluded Weaver and escaped, driving off to the Sheriff's Department. She immediately acquired a gun permit and purchased a .32 automatic revolver and adequate clips.

There was no witness summoned to state that Mrs. Weaver spent the rest of the afternoon in target practice. Nor was the friend called to tell of the struggle in her front yard between Norvella and Thomas. Of the more than twenty customers in the Weaver's Camp bar later in the evening, only two responded for questioning.

Tom Weaver had ambled into the camp and sat at the bar about 10:30 P.M. that night of August 23. Norvella lifted her head and her voice inflection as she gave her account of the shooting:

"When I saw that man come in, I went right to the kitchen where I had hid the gun under a towel. I wrapped it in a fold of my apron, and I went back to the bar. Tom went about armed continually, and he was right handy with a gun. I knew he had come out there to kill me that night. When I passed him, he jostled me and said, 'This is it!' That's when I shot him."

The prosecutor asked, "Did Mr. Weaver have a gun? Is that what he jostled you with?"

Norvella frowned and answered, "I don't know. It could have been his elbow, but I wasn't taking any chances. He had a gun that same afternoon, as I done told you. It was either him or me!"

Lester parried, "But why did you reload the gun even after he was already wounded and lying helpless on the floor?"

Without hesitation she said, "Because he wasn't dead yet!" She had fired four more bullets into the prostrate Tom Weaver after the initial seven missiles had entered his body. She explained, "After I shot him for sure I just sat down and said, 'Call the Sheriff.'"

Her gray-green eyes looked directly at the coroner's jury, and then

24

she was led by her attorney to a front row seat next to an elderly man in shirt sleeves who kept wiping his perspiring face with a blue bandana. I was told that he was Norvella's father, who had come down from Alabama to help her run the Stock Island business.

The coroner's jury returned to the partitioned room, but Hamlin had realized that discussions could be overheard, so he cleared the main room. Markers were placed on coveted seats. One woman took off her shoes to put on her chair. In the interval, the cold drink vendors and the Good Humor Man did a sellout business.

After a half hour of deliberation, the jury and the audience filed back into their places. The foreman, J. Winfield Russell, answered Hamlin's request for a decision with solemn demeanor. "We have duly considered all the facts brought before us. We all agree that this is a case of justifiable homicide, and the shooting was done in self-defense."

Norvella Weaver embraced her father, sobbing in relief. The crowd cheered.

Immediately after the death of Weaver, who operated a small steak house where Rod's Inn was later established, the sign on his place of business was ordered changed. The original read: "Weaver's Sizzling Steaks." The painter was told to paint out the first word on the sign. Through an error, he painted out the last word instead. The sign then read "Weaver's Sizzling."

Local wags quipped, "That's just right! Weaver is sizzling down in hell."

THE CON MAN

The legend of Prince Charming in reverse is the story of Julius F. Stone, Jr., a brilliant man whose luster became tarnished as he progressed toward a career of power and the acquisition of money. He was a native of Ohio, where his father was a wealthy man and a director of Ohio State University in Columbus.

In fact, my Master's Degree diploma from Ohio State was signed by Julius F. Stone, Sr.

Young Stone left his home state and furthered his education at Harvard University. He received a doctorate in organic chemistry in 1926. In 1940, he would earn a law degree at Harvard, according to the late Richard Rovere, who wrote an article on Key West and Stone for the December 15, 1951 issue of *The New Yorker*.

Stone was a millionaire in the Coolidge era when he ventured into the stock market. Came the crash of 1929, and he had lost his first fortune. But he was not at a loss for a job. He became a talented administrator in New York State, doing social welfare work under Harry Hopkins. This link ultimately forged Stone's career in Key West, after Hopkins became one of the President Franklin Roosevelt's chiefs. Eleanor Roosevelt, also a friend of Hopkins, and of Stone through her profound interest in social welfare, likely had influence in Stone's appointment, via Hopkins, as director of the Federal Emergency Relief Administration (FERA) for the Southeastern United States. The territory included Florida, Puerto Rico, and the Caribbean possessions, such as the Virgin Islands.

The important assignment was made in 1933. In 1934 Stone came to Key West to survey his territory, and decide what could be done for the island, which was virtually bankrupt as far as the city government was concerned. Nearly everyone was on relief, with only a few wealthier citizens free of debt, if not of worry.

Although Stone spent much of his time and effort here, he also had duties elsewhere in the vast project, and assistance was needed. A staff of eleven FERA workers was established in Key West.

Stone applied his energy and expertise through 1934 and 1935, and achieved a general cleanup of the town, which had streets piled high with uncollected garbage. He established a WPA division, bringing artists to the island. Among them was Bill Hoffman, who still lives here. Stone got people to paint their homes and fix up property, with the aim of making Key West a resort town that could cash in on its natural attraction as a tourist mecca.

Bold methods furthered the administrator's success in putting Key West back on its financial feet. He declared the island "in the existence of a state of emergency." He ignored standard procedures for a system that was at least on the fringe of being illegal. Stone confessed to writer Rovere that he used FERA funds to subsidize air service to Key West and to get the Casa Marina Hotel back in operation.

These items, and the fact that he risked government funds, should have been clear indication of Stone's later ruthless methods in manipulating other people's money. But, at the moment, there was only a brightening on the horizon of Key West's future. Stone seemed to be a modern knight in impregnable armor. His local nickname was "Kingfish," after the enterprising character on the popular radio show of the times, "Amos and Andy."

One amusing aspect of Stone's efforts was his attempted introduction of the wearing of shorts, as was done in the Bahamas. He set a personal example of donning the abbreviated sportswear, but as far as Conchs were concerned, the innovation was laughable. As Walter Norman pointed out in his book, *Nicknames and Conch Tales*, one Volunteer Work Corps laborer appeared on the job in his underdrawers. Declared he, "If Julius Stone can come to work in his underwear, so can I!"

The front cover of *Florida Motorist* for October 1934 featured Stone's photo along with that of President Franklin D. Roosevelt and Dave Sholtz, Governor of Florida. That year he was approaching middle age. He appeared as a handsome sophisticate, with a black mustache, and a slightly receding hairline over a deep and broad forehead. He looks alert and confident and is posed holding a pen over a sheet of paper. Indeed, his most quoted saying was, "With a stroke of the pen I can give it to you–and with the stroke of a pen, I can take it away.

In following decades, he was to do just that.

Florida Motorist complimented Stone and his staff on rehabilitation of Key West and Monroe County. The editorial page carried a drawing of a rainbow arched over the letters "F.E.R.A." and Governor Sholtz's comment, "The Dawn of a New Era." A declaration by Stone stated that visitors to the island were welcome, but that the FERA would prefer that they not come at all, unless prepared to spend at least three full days. "A shorter trip would be unfair to the visitor, and to Key West", he emphasized.

Endorsements of the plan were made by prominent citizens and businessmen, including William A. Freeman, Allen Cleare, A. Villate, Paul Lumley, and the Porter-Allen Insurance Company. This was a challenging policy, but one which was successful. The parade of tourists began to increase.

Good publicity lifted the gloom which had beset the Keys, and by the time Stone departed in 1935 to engage in WPA troubleshooting elsewhere, realization of his vision was shaping into reality.

After two years more in government service, Stone enrolled in Harvard Law School in 1937. After he had graduated in 1940, he returned to the scene of his FERA triumphs. He set up a law practice here and became a real estate dealer and investment expert, and in a short time he was a leading Key West citizen.

During one period, after he became a member of the Florida Bar, Stone went into partnership with attorney W. Curry Harris. When World War II came along, Harris joined the military service. After the war was over, he returned to Key West to discover that his law practice was non-existent. It had been absorbed by his erstwhile partner. There was, of course, estrangement and bitterness. Harris, however, reestablished himself and became a prominent attorney all over again, with a specialty in town property and deeds. He retired to Sarasota.

Skipping back to the early days of the "Stone Age," as it might be dubbed, Stone formed an association with Dine Beakes, a lawyer from Jacksonville. They purchased part of Boca Chica Beach from Luther Pinder and planned a home division. In 1947 the pair managed to get an okay from Stone's friend, Governor Sholtz, permitting the tearing down of the old Boca Chica Bridge. There was a protest by local people. The beach homes hope did not materialize, but Stone organized another housing development off Rest Beach, and with reputable backing and solid partners the subdivision prospered.

Loans were easily obtainable through Stone's office at an exorbitant rate of interest–twelve percent. A banker explained that, since this was outside the recognized limit, a way around the difficulty was devised. The trick was to lend, say $10,000. But the borrower received only $8,000.

A clever attorney, as well as a sharp businessman, Stone's status in the community was increased by his legal prowess. He was the defense counsel in the sensational 1949 Weaver murder case. He also was attorney for Aerovias Q, the Cuban airline that operated between here and Havana, and he sold stock in the company, as well. He represented a gas company and a grocery market, among other businesses. He doubled in these through investment guidance. This meant extra legal fees for advice and for legal services rendered, not to mention the investment procedure itself.

The list of clients in intermeshing interests is too long to report in full, but here is one example:

In 1949, I bought the gift section of Southernmost Flowers and Gifts, then at 616 Duval Street. The shop owner was Norval Reed, and Stone was his lawyer as well as becoming mine. Eventually, when Reed left Key West for Miami, he sold the flower shop department to my mother, Lila (Mrs. Earle) Raymer, a widow, and Stone handled that transaction, too. We all paid fat fees for Stone's multi-faceted work. In 1951, circumstances—including a death in the family, my mother's return to Pennsylvania, wages for extra help, building repairs, and a rebuilt refrigerator for the florist trade— were too much to sustain without going into debt. A buyer with money to spend wanted the business. Stone put on pressure, and we had to cut our losses and sell at a discount.

A banking official informed me later that it was Stone's habit to take advantage of demand notes and to bring about foreclosure on short notice, not giving a chance for time adjustment.

And so it was with many other persons and businesses. The administration of estates was another field which benefitted Stone. In one case, a young man who had inherited his father's estate found that it "had been administrated out of existence," as his uncle told me.

A curious case came to light in August 1955, when the Public Gas Company was sued by the Keys Bottled Gas Company, doing business as Keys Propane Gas and Marathon Gas. A bill of complaint was filed by Julius Stone, as attorney for the latter. (Stone was also a promoter and had gotten various people to invest in Keys Bottled Gas). In the complaint, Stone alleged that former employees of Keys Bottled Gas had taken records and documents when they shifted companies. He claimed the Public Gas concern refused to return the documents and asked Circuit Court to enjoin the Public Gas Company from "tampering with tanks and damaging bottled gas installations."

But Judge Pat Cannon of Miami denied the injunction and pronounced that the suit failed to prove all the charges. The resulting "scandal" was a discredit to Stone, and more than one person lost invested money.

Stone and his attractive wife, Lee, whose first name was actually

Lucille, had become part of the upper social structure of the town, and they acquired many friends, which of course aided Stone in his monetary ventures. When the Stones bought the former dwelling of novelist Thelma Strabel, who wrote *Reap the Wild Wind*, claim was made that the residence was the true Southernmost House, and that, geographically, the mansion, which is now owned by Hilario Ramos, Sr., was the "Southernmost" in name only.

Ramos Jr., known as "Charlie," hinted that the actual survey was never made. He also said that Stone admitted he designated his abode on South Street, near the corner of Whitehead, as the genuine Southernmost house simply for "commercial enhancement." The hassle disrupted a friendship between the Ramos family and Stone.

Stone juggled all of his diversified financial schemes with wily skill for more than a decade. He was president of the Key West Art and Historical Society along about 1953-1954, and he became a director of the Florida First National Bank. A reputable bank official noted that Julius Stone kept his various investments extremely secret, and no one but he knew exactly what was being transacted.

Ultimately, his wizardly juggling of a wide range of business interests and investments became too complicated. He began to lose control of the precarious balance. In short, money acquired for one thing was put into something entirely different, and some investors sustained losses. In a number of cases invested funds disappeared entirely.

Lillian Lopez, widow of the late Judge Aquilino Lopez Jr., who was closely associated with Stone for a long period in the early years, said that her husband's law practice was separate from Stone's, and that, although they were together for some time in real estate, Stone and Lopez broke off business relations and severed even friendship when it was revealed that Stone was engaged in suspicious financial activity.

"My husband was upset and decided that Julius was too much of a dealer," Lillian Lopez said. "He became a judge and was a dedicated man in judiciary matters, while Stone continued to mix law and investment involvements."

The roster of "victims" lengthened. Among the losers were Frances Edwards, who operated the Banana Tree Grill; Ruth Alfred who owned a trailer park and bought the Flame Restaurant; Gertrude Ricketts, who operated a private school (she later married Cmdr. Ray Byrns); Alice Bredin, artist; Ethel Decker, a crippled florist who got caught up through mortgaged property in Mexico;

and Dr. Aubrey Hamilton and his wife, Belle. Stone was godfather to the Hamiltons' children, but even that friendship was violated when Stone demanded several thousand dollars more than Hamilton had put into the building of a semi-supermarket.

Sometime, somewhere in this mid-1950's chronicle of wheeler-dealer expansiveness, two widows fell prey to the complicated designs of Stone's financial intrigue. The attention of federal authorities was brought to bear on the situation.

In 1955 the Stones erected a new home in Trinidad, Cuba, and numerous friends from Key West, including Adeline and P.J. Ross, Lillian and Aquilino Lopez, and Burt and Betty Garnett, were invited to inspect it. It was no secret that the Stones intended to establish another residence out of the country.

Despite the ongoing revolution in Cuba, the Stones went ahead with plans to leave the United States. They liquidated holdings here and began moving possessions to Trinidad. Fidel Castro took over Cuba on January 1, 1959, marching into Havana, and at first his triumph was met with approval by sympathizers here.

In the summer of 1959, Stone was still a director at Florida First National. His picture was published in the *Key West Citizen* on July 1, 1959, as a member of the Grievance Committee. Ironically this group was set up by the Florida Bar to monitor the ethics of lawyers in the organization.

Meantime, bank officials began to ease Stone out of his bank directorship, and, although it can't be verified, Stone's business ventures, or rather misadventures, continued to be probed. I spoke with at least twenty Key West people, and all of them agreed that he was on a "wanted" list and seriously in debt.

Charlie Ramos had a note from Stone, dated September 12, 1959, in which Stone wrote that he and his wife were busy packing in preparation for the move to Cuba. Lee Stone went back and forth, supposedly on Aerovias Q missions and once to pick up valuables which belonged to Oscar Morales, Cuban Consul in Key West. But Lee was also transferring personal property, documents and funds.

Now for the final severance move, and Julius Stone's partial restitution of debts or taxes:

He arranged secret contact with Old Island Realty Company for transfer of the deed to his home on South Street. His wife went to the consulate's office in Havana, where Consul Wayne Gilchrist executed the deed for the property for which Lucille (Lee) Stone signed January 19, 1960.

The stamp value was duly registered later and was recorded as

$45,000. The house was purchased from the Stones by Granville and Evelyn Smith, of 1120 Von Phister Street. The warranty deed was signed "Julius F. Stone, Jr.," but no address was given for him.

Shortly after the official registration of the sale in the Monroe County Courthouse, Stone flew to Key West in a small plane and landed at the Key West International Airport.

The popular version is that he did not leave the plane at all, and that the exchange of the deed for a prescribed sum of money took place aboard the plane. The late Aileen Williams of Old Island Realty was the courier.

However, Stone *did* leave the plane, and *did* set foot in Key West. First of all, he was seen off the plane and at the airport here by Anne (Mrs. Guy) Carleton. She says he did not speak to her but turned around and vanished in the terminal.

Second, Mrs. Aquilino Lopez asserts that the plane sustained mechanical trouble, and Stone was obliged to stop overnight at a motel. He notified the judge and his wife of the sale of the South Street house. He took off early the next day, flying out of Key West for the last time. He was in possession of the purchase money.

The plane may have been the one he owned privately, which was flown by a special pilot. During a summer vacation in the early '60s, *Key West Citizen* Chief Photographer Don Pinder went to Nassau in the Bahamas. It was then known that Stone, if not an actual fugitive, was being investigated for his fast "deals." Pinder met Stone on Bay Street in Nassau, and they had a drink together in a bar. Stone said that he was temporarily living on an Out Island of the Bahamas. He did not disclose the exact location.

The relationship between the Castro government and the United States became more troubled. As 1960 advanced, Americans were in disfavor in Cuba. The city of Trinidad, as an outskirt locality, was considered dangerous, so the Stones left for the comparative safety of Havana. They operated an antique furniture store on the famed Prado, but only for a short time. They retreated to Jamaica, where Lee died in 1963. She had been a beautiful woman, noted for her charm. The day I met her, she was wearing brightly colored ribbons braided into her hair, Mexican style, and impressed me with her genuine warmth of personality.

There is a gap in Julius Stone's history following Lee's demise in 1963. Little or nothing is known of his maneuvers between then and May 1965. It was then that Anne Carleton once more, unexpectedly, encountered the expatriate.

She was getting ready for a coach tour to Scotland and was standing in line at the American Express in London when she saw Stone. They renewed acquaintances, and he told her that he had been married the day before to Christine Beakes.

The attractive Christine, widow of Dine Beakes, Stone's law partner of years past, was known as the Hibiscus Lady, because of the blossoms she wore in her hair. She lived in a house on the waterfront during World War II and was at one time suspected of being an enemy spy. This rumor was unconfirmed and was denied by people who knew her well. But, as usual, this island was a hotbed of gossip, and Christine never lived down the suspicion.

The newly marrieds were staying with an aristocratic English friend, and were leaving the next day for Spain. Anne told Julius she wanted to speak with her old friend, Christine, and he gave her the telephone number. After a conversation with the bride, Anne went on her tour and the Stones went to their new destination.

There communication ceased.

Hilario Ramos, Sr., said that the Stones lived in Spain for a time, then took up residence on Majorca, a resort island off the Spanish Coast.

Within the next two years, wanderlust, perhaps compulsory, took over again, and Stone, presumably accompanied by his second wife, travelled on toward the East. The aimed-for destination is not known, for in 1967 Julius F. Stone, Jr., died in Australia.

Details of Stone's death are vague. It was said that he died of a heart attack. The news did not reach Key West until he had been dead for a long time.

His only child was a daughter, Julia, who was graduated from Bennington, and married twice. Her whereabouts is not known.

And so ends the Prince Charming saga, on the other side of the world, far from Stone's homeland. A story much like the central character in *Man Without a Country*.

PADDY WAGON PATROL

According to official record, when Harry S. Truman was President of the United States, he spent eleven working vacations on the island, staying on the Naval Station at the Little White House. His arrivals were always signaled by an advance squad of Secret Service men, who filtered into town before the main presidential party, and scouted the area. More Secret Service agents would accompany Truman's retinue. They protected the President, his family, and any VIPs, around the clock.

One Cuban-American resident and his wife delighted in entertaining the Secret Service men and special U.S. Marines on duty. The host and hostess always provided a lavish Cuban-style feast at their home. Since all the governmental watchdogs could never be present at the same time, arrangements were made so that the honored guests could attend the festivity in relays.

Preparation for the festivity began in early morning. A suckling pig was put on a spit to roast over a trench-pit dug in the back yard. The pork was cooked all day, basted at regular intervals. All sorts of Cuban dishes, plain and fancy, were also on the list: arroz con polio, paella, frijoles negros, picadillo, yucca, and on through to flan and tropical fruit served on ice.

As for drinks, an amazing array of cocktails and frothy rum concoctions were dispensed from an outside bar on the grounds, as well as from a bar set up in the dining room near the buffet table.

I arrived for the second phase of the evening escorted by a Navy lieutenant whom I had known for several years. He was aboard a visiting destroyer, which was here for Truman's visit. Luke, his nickname, had once been stationed in Key West and was well known to most of the politicos and other military officers present at the fete.

As the evening became night, the food was consumed at an appreciative rate, so the hostess brought on a huge turkey which had to be carved. My escort volunteered to perform the task, and did so with professional skill. The hostess was so grateful that she and her husband presented him with a bottle of aged, rare brandy.

Luke was elated with all the compliments and generously offered to share the brandy, which he had opened. Since most of the crowd had been quaffing rum, only two or three sipped some of the fine liquor, but Luke began nipping frequently. I couldn't pry him away from his scene of triumph for nearly two hours. By that time it was past midnight and the party was breaking up.

I had worn a long-skirted evening gown, since we had planned to go dancing at Fort Taylor. Luke was not in uniform, having donned a pair of dark slacks and shirt. Under the circumstances, I thought it best to forget any further expeditions for the night. In fact, I even suggested getting a taxi and leaving the car where he had parked it near the site of the party.

But Luke's machismo had ballooned, and he insisted that the idea was insulting. Rather than stir up his antagonism in front of so many people, I got into the ancient black Packard he had borrowed, and we set out on a somewhat erratic course for my cottage near Solares Hill, around the corner from Weintraub's grocery where Angela Street joins Elizabeth.

There had been a rash of prowlers in the vicinity, so there were police lookouts posted in the neighborhood. One of them stood watch from a second story balcony at the store. Of course we were unaware of this vigilance, or of the accompanying police van nearby.

We pulled up on Angela Street in front of my place, and Luke jockeyed to park the big car in a space too small for it. He started to make room by backing against the front of an auto parked behind him. In so doing, he banged into the other vehicle, creating a loud noise in the still night.

The sound of the contact alerted the law.

By the time I had climbed out of the front seat and reached the safety (I thought) of the sidewalk, only a few yards from my own front door, we were converged upon by two burly cops, one from the patrol wagon which had swung around the corner, and the other who had come down from the store balcony. The patrolmen approached the Packard. Luke was still behind the wheel. The motor was running, so he couldn't claim he was parked and not driving.

"Let's see your driver's license," demanded the cop, leaning in the car window. Luke hauled out his wallet and searched it to no avail. Then he shuffled the contents of the glove compartment. Still no license.

He mumbled, "I must have left it in my other trousers aboard ship."

By that time, the policeman had evidently got a strong whiff of Luke's brandy-scented breath. He ordered Luke out of the car. Unfortunately, when Luke opened the door, the brandy bottle rolled out on the street from the car floor. The bottle was about a third full. The policeman retrieved it and announced, "How's that for positive evidence?" He reached in and removed the ignition keys, then again ordered Luke out of the car.

This was accomplished with complaints and great effort, until Luke stood teetering back and forth on the road. He was nudged to the sidewalk beside me. There he assumed an arrogant attitude and intoned, "Do you happen to know who I am? I am a naval officer and I demand release."

I kicked Luke in the ankle and warned, "Shut up!" I didn't know the cops, but I could sense the rising antagonism between Luke and his captors.

The patrolman asked, "What did you say?" He glared at me.

"I said 'Shut up,' sir, but I meant it for Luke, not you," I replied.

The policeman snorted and brandished his night stick. He gestured toward the waiting Black Maria and commanded "Get in! Both of you!"

The back doors were swung wide, and we climbed the mounting steps to enter the dark interior. Inside there were two long, wooden benches lining the sides of the wagon. The seats were smooth, hard and slippery. There were no hand grips. The doors were slammed shut, the driver started with a lurch, and we slid halfway down the bench toward the front of the van. It was almost pitch black inside. We couldn't see out, but from the tilt of the vehicle I realized we were going down Angela toward Duval Street.

We slid along the seats toward the front, then back again as the wagon came to an abrupt halt. The rear doors were yanked open, and I glimpsed just enough of the outside setting to know we had stopped alongside the Tropics, a rowdy night spot, a the corner of Angela and Duval Streets. This was later the site of the highly respectable Lowell C. Restaurant.

Within seconds, a mob of white-hatted sailors appeared, shoved along by members of the Shore Patrol. Evidently, they had been fighting, for their uniforms were in disarray and faces battered, but they were in a laughing mood as they stumbled aboard and fell onto the benches.

One young serviceman leered at me, shoved his round hat over an eye and saluted. "Hi, babe!" he said.

At that point Luke assumed his officer's dignity and retorted, "How dare you speak to her like that? She is a lady!"

The sailor grinned and retorted, "Yeah? Then what's she doing in the paddy wagon?"

"You've got a point there, Bubba," I said as the van jolted off, all the "inmates" slipping and sliding on the slippery seats.

A guard was balanced on the van steps for the rest of the journey and, as the doors were slightly ajar, I could see out along the route. We rattled to our destination, the Old City Hall at Ann Street and Greene.

The police department offices were on street level, and we were just a stone's throw from the *Key West Citizen* office. I hoped none of my staff colleagues were hanging around the locality. I thought that I might be able to ease into headquarters undetected, if you will excuse the expression.

Small chance of that! The wagon doors were slammed wide open, and the sailors scrambled out, then formed a double line through which I was obliged to pass. They bowed in ragged array and made comments such as "Make way for her ladyship," and "Royal escorts at your service."

I decided I might as well face the situation with humor. Assuming a mock haughty pose, I gathered up the hem of my gown and swept regally into the station.

In the outer office I recognized the police lieutenant on desk duty. He looked shocked as he saw me and exclaimed, "What are you doing here?"

Glad to see a member of the force with whom I was acquainted, I launched into a hurried explanation about saying "Shut-up!" to my date, but not to the arresting officer.

The desk official studied me for a few seconds. "Okay," he said. "You can wait in the chief's office." I was ushered into the adjacent room with a noisy background sendoff from the sailors. Comments included, "Bye-bye, Queenie, give 'em the royal what for!" and "Good night, your ladyship," plus some bawdy remarks which don't bear repeating.

I waited for at least a half hour while the booking process went on in the outer office. The door was half open and I could see and hear what was going on. The "disorderly dozen" were relegated to Shore Patrol control. Then the assistant to the Chief of Police came into the inner room. He said, "I want you to witness this."

Luke was brought in, glaring and belligerent, by a policeman. The chief's assistant said, "Now watch this closely. We give a few tests to determine degree of intoxication."

First, he tossed a dime on the floor and ordered Luke to pick it up. Luke, who had sobered up a little, sneered and snarled, "Make it a fifty-cent piece and maybe I will." He added, "I can't walk a straight line, either, so don't bother to have me try. So what's next?"

It was to be a breathalyzer test. But that didn't come off either. Luke was so inebriated he failed to blow up the balloon.

The detective in charge of the demonstration pointed out with heavy sarcasm, "Your lieutenant claims he forgot his license. Let me tell you, he has a record of repeated drunken driving, and his license was suspended for a year. That was several months ago."

So it was back to the drunk tank for Luke, and a police officer was assigned to drive me home. As we left the station I spotted a Navy security officer and managed to tell him about Luke's plight. I suggested he get in touch with the executive officer of Luke's ship, since I thought things were going to be tough for Luke. I learned later that this was done.

Within a few days, Luke was transferred to San Diego. No story concerning the bizarre episode was printed in the newspaper, for which I was thankful.

A long time after the experience, I couldn't resist inserting a cryptic line in my column, "Conch Chowder." It was merely an oblique reference on a list of items due for city improvement.

"Recommended: Better padded paddy wagons."

NUDIST COLONY

A condominium for nudists has been planned for the Tampa area, according to a news story. Everybody has some knowledge, chiefly secondhand, about nudist colonies. Most colonies, outside of European nudist-accepted resorts, are secluded, set in out-of-the-way locations on private property sites. Now there seems to be a new trend where there will be a concentration under one roof of people sans clothing.

I can't help but wonder if the rules of the usual nudist circles will be applied, even to workers on the property. Nobody, but nobody, as a slogan used to go, will be permitted to wear anything, not even "thong" suits, and the ruling would be strict, governing bellhops, switchboard operators, elevator attendants, dining and kitchen staff members–although cooks and chefs might possibly be permitted to don protective aprons while slaving over hot skillets.

It is likely that employees ordered to discard uniforms would have to undergo unusual training in order to become accustomed to being uncostumed. This might result in disclosure of otherwise hidden talents. The ability, for instance, to remain poker-faced even with an over-all royal flush, and to retain calm composure under all circumstances dealing with customers also nude.

One supposes that the exception to the no-covering order would cover doormen, since they would be in view of the outside population. Of course, an inner screen stage could be established, just beyond the outer portals. Anyway, a great deal of in-depth speculation on the problems of a nudist condominium may be viewed with the naked eye. (How else?)

A lot of hilarious incidents are bound to occur under stripped conditions. Remember a movie starring the late Peter Sellers as the bashful hero who wanders into a nudist paradise? He encounters a hell of complications and a burden of duress because his garments were taken from him under the ruling that no clothing could be worn on the nudist camp property.

Also remember that, thirty years ago, the general attitude in Key West, either ingrained or acquired, was "No nudes is good nudes." So eyebrows were raised when mention was made of a secret new nudist movement, an out-of-cover undercover attitude, by a small group led by Kit and Kay Lawrence, pseudonyms for writer Larry

Karns and his wife Tomi. Larry was an excellent writer, artist and photographer. Tomi was a model and photographer, and also ran their studio. Both contributed to top national nudist publications, and had belonged to nudist clubs in Cleveland, Ohio, and elsewhere.

As advocates of nudism, stressing the health aspects, fresh air and sunshine, without any hampering apparel, the Karnses formed the nucleus of a local pioneer nudist retreat on an uninhabited island just off Key West. They began recruiting fans through friends elsewhere, who came here on visits, and by persuading the Key West liberal and more adventurous inhabitants to join them.

As I became better acquainted with Larry and Tomi, starting with Larry's occasional humorous contributions to my "Conch Chowder" column in the *Key West Citizen*, we became close friends. Over a period of several months I was finally persuaded to inspect the nudist beachhead in its hideaway location. I had gleaned favorable impressions from several guests whose reports were glowing. "All very peaceful and charming," I was told. "You get used to the atmosphere without any problem."

The real persuader which fired my inclination to try a nudist setting was provided unintentionally by my friend and erstwhile journalism colleague at Ohio State University, then a celebrity and night club columnist, Earl Wilson. He often quipped that the class of 1930 produced not one, but two saloon editors, an unusual achievement for such a staid seat of learning. He described his visit to a nudist colony, and I decided to emulate him. I talked about the experiment with Larry and Tomi, and they guaranteed that for the initial visit, at least, I would be the only guest at their camp that day.

Arrangements were made for me to go along on a Sunday. The day for the rendezvous dawned bright and sun-filled. There was more than a hint that progressing hours would be steaming with midsummer heat, and the thought of swimming, unencumbered by a bathing suit, had its appeal. I had been swimming under cover of night back in more innocent days when a group of "marrieds" at Antioch College risked reputations by going to swim in the pool below The Gorge, a rugged ravine off the campus. We felt daring, although we dived in wearing swim suits and took them off only after nightfall. Despite claims of all nudists that their inclination is health-motivated, I thought the custom smacked of exhibitionism. I also was still inhibited by Edwardian upbringing. I had discarded most of the prudery and considered myself liberated, as it were, but not to the point of public "display."

40

At any rate, I arrived at the Karns household that morning clad in a modest one-piece swim suit and equipped with bath towels, a large beach towel, bathing cap, suntan oil, and what I hoped was a look of nonchalance. We set off up the highway in the Karns auto, towing their small outboard boat on its trailer. To this day, I don't know where the turnoff began, but it was somewhere off U.S. 1, near Boca Chica. We jolted over a barely visible track down to the water's edge.

The little craft was loaded to the gunwales with food supplies, camping equipment, an ice container, and beach articles, as well as a bailing bucket, oars, and a long pole for getting through shallow places. We all wore thick-soled footgear–a wise measure, since eventually we had to wade along narrow, bush-lined passages and shallow channels strewn with sea urchins, sharp rocks and shells.

Byron, a 75-pound Dalmatian belonging to the Karns menage was aboard, too. He stood up in the prow, barking constantly, so there wasn't much chance for conversational exchange even when we glided along smoothly under motor power. And that was only for a limited period of about half an hour. We first wound around in a labyrinth of deep, shady channels, then reached more shallow waterways and had to climb out to lighten the load. We pushed the boat with the keel just grazing the bottom. Only Byron remained aboard in majestic dogdom. Mosquitoes and midges, or "no-see-ums," soon discovered us, and we frequently stopped guiding and shoving the boat through the trickle of sustaining water to roll in welcome wetness.

At long last, we reached an opening into deeper water and clambered back into the now freely floating hull. The outboard resumed its rhythmic pulse and we putt-putted along, swerving to the north on the border of the Atlantic. After a few minutes, helmsman Karns called out in mock dramatics, "Land ahoy!" He shut off the motor and poled us into a charming little cove. We nosed up a small, tidy, white sand beach, bordered with buttonwood and mangrove and unidentified bushes. The vista was lovely and secluded with just the peaceful arc of beach facing open and outward to the ocean.

As soon as the boat touched the shore, Byron leaped overboard and went racing inland. We followed, jumping into the foot or so of lapping waves and dragging the boat up on the slight slope of the beach. Larry secured it to a large stake which had been driven deep into the sands on a previous trip.

We started to unload our paraphernalia. I assembled items to take ashore. My back was turned as I bent over the stern picking up gear, and so I failed to see my hosts carry their first burdens up to the camp site. When I turned around I was startled. My hosts were there, stark naked.

I knew this was going to happen, but somehow the abruptness of the confrontation was unnerving. I picked up a box of table utensils and was about to step over the side of the boat. I was still wearing my swim suit.

"Oh, no you don't!" Larry commanded. "You are now in nudist territory and you can't set foot here without removing your suit. The rules are strict, as we warned you. Off with your suit!" He twirled his mustache and tugged at his matching black goatee. Tomi added, "C'mon. You know the rules were set in advance. Don't be so silly!"

So I slowly peeled off my bathing suit and girded up my loins, as they say about acts of courage. Except mine were ungirded. In desperation I grabbed a pile of toweling and the utensil container. Holding the stuff in my arms, clutched to my front, I trudged toward the camping point.

Under a buttonwood tree, there was a trestle table flanked by two long benches. The tree and leafy bushes provided screening from the sunlight, but not from the eyes of my companions. Tomi called, "Just drop that stuff on the table. We'll go back for more."

Reluctantly, I released my shield of towels and whirled back to the boat. Tomi and I lugged the portable icebox to the table. Larry was busy setting up the grill over a hollowed-out pit. Tomi and I struggled to raise the sun umbrella and finally succeeded. We were perspiring after that effort, so I happily ran down to the water again and plunged in. I swam around and around until I was exhausted. Then, glad of the partial concealment afforded by the wavelets, I flopped down on my stomach and rested my head on my forearms, relaxed.

But not for long! The Dalmatian decided he wanted to romp and came thrashing around. He kept pushing me with his paws and, to avoid being drowned in the less than a foot of sea, I scrambled to my feet and retreated further toward camp center where I again stretched out, backside sunny side up.

Byron remained at a distance then, far more interested in the preparations for eating. Larry squatted in the sand using his left hand to brush off insects and his right hand to toast hotdogs above the grill fire. Tomi began removing food from the hamper.

I felt obligated to help, of course, even if it meant shuffling about exposed to full view. But when the meal was ready and all articles were set in place, I sat on the edge of the bench opposite my hosts and slid down as far as possible without disappearing beneath the table, thus concealing myself from the upper chest down.

Have you ever tried to eat with your chin in your plate and your body in an exaggerated slump? Well, don't. It simply doesn't work! I kept slopping ketchup on my chin and dropping potato salad on my bronchial region. Tomi and Larry howled with laughter. After the futile try, overcome by all that pre-luncheon activity, I finally swallowed my scruples and sat up to swallow my luncheon goodies.

After topping everything off with cookies and cold drinks, we decided to explore the perimeter of the island. I maneuvered so that I walked behind Tomi and Larry. We picked up shells and bits of driftwood, and examined the few wild flowers we discovered. But the sun's rays thrust spears of tropical heat with such intensity that we soon turned back to the shadier landing area. We lolled there for an hour, allowing time for the picnic repast to digest, before taking a final swim. Ironically, I scanned a book called *The Sun Was My Undoing.*

At this point Byron set off a barrage of watchdog explosives, barking furiously. He had been wading around a bend of shoreline and came bounding back toward us with tremendous uproar. Larry motioned Tomi and me into the bushes with our towels, and he stood guard at the cove wrapped in his own towel. I could see over the top of my hiding niche and so beheld a sailboat with half a dozen persons aboard approaching. Larry quickly retrieved a big red-lettered sign from the dinghy and held it aloft. The boat came about and sailed away again.

I examined the sign after the crisis was past. In big glaring red letters it read: "Private Property. No Trespassing!" But I think it was Byron's ferocious stay-away warning which actually scared off the intruders.

We emerged from our leafy bowers with a penalty–mosquito bites! There had been no time to snatch up insect repellent.

We decided to call it a day (What a day!). Besides, the suntan ointment had been used up and I had already begun to feel the effects of imprudent prolonged exposure to the sun's rays, mostly on the protruding portions of my rear anatomy, unaccustomed as it was to public peeking.

We made the return journey without incident, wearing our swim outfits. I took a great deal of kidding about my behavior and attempts to foil the law of nudist gatherings. It was indeed laughable, I agreed.

But the next day the adventure wasn't so funny. It had become a burning issue. After a restless night applying sunburn remedies, I appeared at the *Citizen* office Monday morning, as usual. But I did not have the blues. I had the reds–red hots! I wished I could type a la Hemingway–that is, standing up. It was torture to sit down. My posterior had developed two enormous hand-sized blisters–and they had burst.

In mid-afternoon I gave up and went to see my physician, Dr. Charles Morrison, ex-Navy. He took one look at my southern over-exposure and exclaimed, "What in the blazes have you been up to? (A choice phrase under the conditions!) You have one of the worst cases of broiled buttocks I have ever seen!"

The treatment for the "toasted hams" went on for two weeks. For the first five days I had to lie on my stomach and do everything else standing up. I missed work and spent many hours applying non-friction salve and bandages that wouldn't stay in place.

Needless to say, I never again visited the site of my unseating discomfort. Nor did I write about the nudist adventure, by request of my boss. I was glad to comply out of sheer embroiled embarrassment (there's a pun in that). As for the pioneering spirit for a consecrated and concentrated nudist establishment, it faded with only a few devoted followers adhering, mostly from out of town, and most friends of the Karnses. Larry later moved away from the area and his land lease expired.

In recent years, Key West has had a few nude streakers, and incidents of undraped persons lurking off the shores of Christmas Tree (Wisteria) Island. Also some rugged individuals have capered in the surf at various beach side resorts and in hotel pools. In fact, we have one resort, restaurant attached, that has allowed topless swimming in the pool on the premises.

But a true nudist settlement was never established here.

Perhaps the Tampa region condominium will fire up some naked aspirations.

CUBAN VIEW

During the autumn of 1949 and the winters of 1950 to 1952, I had a gift section in the Southernmost Flowers and Gifts store at 616 Duval. The florists, Paul Baron and Norval Reed, had no delivery truck, so they hired taxis to deliver orders at a cost of fifty cents per errand. This doesn't seem like much money as fares go today, but back then it was considered a quite adequate sum. As a result, there were always three or four taxicabs parked on Duval Street in front of the shop, not only for on-call delivery business, but to pick up passengers in the area.

Every morning, when I arrived to take care of the gift department, the cab drivers exchanged friendly greetings with me. After I had reported on the job, they were available and eager to gossip on town doings. The comments were always amusing and lively. I was entranced with the asides and observations of the drivers who delivered their ideas in fractured Spanish-Cubanese-English, which, in itself, was intriguing.

On one memorable morning, the taximen parked out front were animatedly talking and gesturing dramatically when I appeared. The cabbies were engrossed in a feature article in a magazine published in Havana. Photos illustrated the text. The cabbies buttonholed me, showed me the publication, and spiced up the original account with individual annotations. "Come see," demanded one of the drivers. "You read Spanish? If not, I will explain." He waved the magazine at me, eyes glittering with excitement.

The sensational report in the slick-cover publication concerned a theme which might be regarded as a more earthy version of the opera *Carmen*. It concerned cigar factory workers on the fringe of Havana. The woman in the case was a "stripper." Not the burlesque variety, but a tobacco leaf stripper who prepared strips of big-leaf tobacco for the outer layers in cigar rolling.

There was still a certain amount of glamour attached to cigar-making, and Key West had maintained a deep interest in the industry, although the large cigar-making factories, which once helped put Key West on the map as a wealthy city, had long-since moved to Tampa due to labor problems.

After I had opened the gift counter, I strolled out to the sidewalk to learn what had aroused the readers. I knew enough Spanish to read the story and captions with no difficulty.

A driver, a Senor Blanco, as I remember, thrust the Havana magazine at me and stood by impatiently while I slowly read the text. It was a harrowing report about an eighteen-year-old girl who worked in the cigar factory, which also employed her seducer, a young man who was a "sorter." He was expert at separating the different kinds of tobacco leaves used in various types of cigars.

The background narrative pointed out that the girl had come from a Province of Cuba and was not used to sophisticated city life. Her parents were old-fashioned farmers in the back country. This was, of course, before the reign of Fidel Castro. At that time, under the dictatorship of Batista, there were no reforms and no alleviations for suppressed women, let alone consideration of women's rights and claims.

According to the article, the girl entered into an affair with the young man with deep love on her part and momentary affection on his. He kept promising her that they would marry, but the wedding was put off on one pretext after another. They lived together, but there was no coveted wedding band on the girl's hand.

And she had become pregnant. In fact, Inez, as she was called, was approaching the final month of her pregnancy. At the clinic, the doctor told her she would deliver within three weeks, perhaps sooner.

That night, Inez made a plea to Gabriel, her lover, asking that they get married immediately so that the baby could be born in wedlock. It was important to Inez, who was Catholic, that the baby should have a proper name. And it was equally important to her that the label of illegitimacy be erased even at such a late date.

Her plea was dismissed with a shrug. Gabriel left her weeping on her knees and wandered out for an evening with a crony who liked to drink and play dominoes. There was also a vivacious tourista, who had a car and who was willing to foot the bills when she and the handsome Gabriel made the rounds at night clubs and casinos. They had met at one of the lesser night spots down on the waterfront when the woman was sightseeing with friends. It may seem improbable, but back in the late 1940s and early 1950s, such encounters were not unusual. Lots of women visitors from the United States came to Cuba for casual romantic adventure. In fact, there were even "houses" which provided stud service as well as maintaining escortage for an evening.

Gabriel, having glimpsed a pleasurable world, was thinking of joining one of the escort establishments, and was even so bold as to

46

tell his amorata that he wasn't interested in bonds of matrimony, forthcoming offspring or not. He sauntered out that night, leaving the distraught Inez to contemplate her dismal fate, and her double rejection, not only by her lover, but by her parents, who were severe judges of her behavior.

While she brooded alone, Inez decided that another wrong made a right. In the little house where she lived with Gabriel, the girl made up her embittered mind to revenge the wrong which had been done her. All this was in the tradition of the past, a leftover from the days when Cuban damsels, even in Key West, were accompanied by *duennas*.

Obviously, Inez had escaped the watchfulness of a guardian. But she was still in the mental clutches of the old standard set of morals.

All through the evening, Inez contemplated her situation. It was rumored that she consumed a quantity of rum as solace while the slow hours dragged. Near dawn, Gabriel finally staggered home. He tore off his clothing and fell naked into the big brass bed he shared with Inez. In a short while, he snored, oblivious to any stirring on the part of his bed companion.

But stir she did. Bolstered by the rum, but not really drunk, Inez waited to make sure that Gabriel was sunk in exhausted slumber.

Then she went quietly to the kitchen where she kept her implements for her job as a tobacco leaf cutter.

She selected one tool of her trade. The nearest translation, I believe, is "curvette." The instrument has only one deep blade, very keen, imbedded in a wooden holder, which is slightly rounded and fits into a hand grip with precision.

Inez picked up the curvette and returned to the bedroom where Gabriel lay spread-eagled on the bare mattress, sound asleep.

She later testified that she was sobbing and hysterical when she accomplished what she set out to do. She completely emasculated Gabriel in one sure swipe of the curved knife.

Neighbors in the next door tenement heard the horrendous scream as Gabriel was castrated. They rushed into the apartment in time to stop Inez from slashing her own wrists with the same curvette, and to summon aid for Gabriel.

A neighbor with some medical training stanched the flow of blood. An ambulance was summoned, and Gabriel, still in a half drunken stupor, was carted off to a hospital. Inez, also in a state of shock, was transported to jail, pending the fate of her drastically mutilated lover. There was nothing left of any aspect of the man's masculinity. The magazine displayed a facial study of the pregnant Inez, head raised defiantly. She glared directly into the camera lens with huge, brilliant eyes.

The taximan who examined the photo with me waved his hand in a gesture of sweeping admiration. He stated, "Ah, a woman of much spirit!"

A second photo accompanied the story. A wan-faced Gabriel lay in a hospital bed, eyes closed in sad resignation. Senor Blanco shook his head as he contemplated the caption under the magazine photo. It read: "Gabriel—in hospital fighting for life."

His ultimate query: "Yeah? Why the hell should he fight at all, after what happened to him?"

Another favorite story related by the gabby cabby who loved to collect and hold an audience of fellow drivers, or anyone hanging around the vicinity of 616 Duval Street, is a monkey business tale.

It is best repeated in dialect, but the staccato speech pattern is impossible to reproduce in print. Readers will have to supply some imagination, with accent, for a true demonstration of the narration. Johnny dePoo, a former City Commissioner, was an expert at this, and he, too, was fond of describing the incident.

A Key West man named Arturo owned a dainty female monkey. He referred to the pet as his "Girl Rhesus," or just "Girl" for short.

The owner was a sensitive fellow, attuned to feelings of animals as well as human beIngs. He often talked with friends about his pet. She had become moody and no longer frolicked in her cage or chattered at him in simian language, which Arturo purported to understand, at least in part. He would clasp a hand to his heart, operatic style, and shake his head sadly, remarking, "Ah, my poor little one! She is lonely. She is longing for a boyfriend, I am sure. But since she came from Cuba, it is most important that she meet a suitable mate from her own district. He must be a Cuban-born Rhesus, who speaks to her in his native way."

Despite a veterinarian's assurance that any healthy Rhesus male monkey would do, Arturo insisted on applying his theory of a romantic liaison from the "Pearl of the Caribbean," as Havana was known. This happened nearly a decade before Castro took over Cuba, when the ties between Key West and Havana were silken smooth, as well as binding.

Arturo had close relatives just across the ninety miles of tropic waters separating the islands. He got in touch with one of them, and arrangements were made to purchase and import a young companion for "Girl." It involved extra money and pull to get permission to admit the alien animal, plus local influence, but Arturo was determined to provide the best for his favored pet. All was achieved in due time, and a fine specimen of the wanted breed was brought over on a private fishing boat and installed in a cage close to that of Girl Rhesus.

She was curious about him but not overexcited. She leaped nimbly from bar to bar in her own quarters and peered through the wire, surveying the monkey to whom Arturo referred discreetly as "my monkey's fiancé."

"Fiancé" became the newcomer's name. He was inspected by all of Arturo's friends and relatives. "Fiancé" received the stamp of approval from the onlookers, if not from "Girl," who began sulking in a corner as if resentful of the admiration and attention given her intended.

The consulting veterinarian told Arturo that time was rapidly approaching when it would be well to introduce the pair on more intimate terms than mere proximity of caged-confines. He advised caution, and that a standby guard squad be in attendance at the preliminaries. After all, Rhesus Girl was small, demure, and a little timid. Fiancé was apparently a monkey with machismo; he was bold and active and had a dashing manner.

Preparations were made for the day of beckoning—with reckoning. The individual cages were placed in adjacent sites, and the main cage doors fitted together, but still closed. A slide adjustment was made so that the doors could be drawn up simultaneously, leaving an open passageway between the wired-over enclosures.

Men stood by with sturdy sticks to interfere should Fiancé take it into his head to get rough with the bride-to-be. A few pacifying bananas were put into each cage. While "Girl" and "Fiancé" began peeling the fruit and feasting, the guard contingent cautiously advanced and stood at the ready.

The entrances to the respective cages were lifted. The watchers were on the alert for any fast moves on the part of the imported beau.

Still, they were unprepared for what happened.

Girl finished her two bananas in short order. Through the joined cage openings, she could see Fiancé slowly consuming his share of the goodies, with the assurance of a king dining in solitary leisure. Girl hesitated only momentarily. Then she scampered from her cage into his and grabbed up a portion of the last banana which lay before him.

Not content with snatching up the leftovers, Rhesus Girl looked up into the surprised visage of the male monkey, snarled, and inserted her nimble-fingered paws right into his jaws, which were crammed with the banana he was chewing. She popped out what he had in his mouth and popped it into her own. Then she grimaced at him menacingly and scooted back into her own cage with the unpeeled loot. There she devoured the stolen banana and assumed a superior pose.

As for Fiancé, he cowered in an abject state of shock, retreating to a cage perch. There he huddled until the doors of both cages were closed and the cages moved apart.

Later reports revealed that Fiancé never recovered from the assault on his male dignity. He never approached Rhesus Girl again. She, however, recovered from her emotional retreat and was once more a merry monkey.

Poor Fiancé lived only another six months or so.

Arturo remained loyal to his domineering female pet. The taximan, who spun out this caperish maneuver for me, snorted with indignation. "That Rhesus Girl became just like an American woman. She—*she, not he,* is the boss of the house. Pah!" And he spat.

This happened before the disputed days of woman's lib, of course. Nobody was monkeying around with that issue back then.

LA SEMANA ALEGRA — FIASCO

"Why doesn't Key West put on an annual pageant based on its colorful history?" That question was asked me by a friend who had seen several such events in various parts of the country, including the Cherokee Indian pageant set in the Great Smokies. The answer probably lies with the staging of a local pageant some years ago. The effort was tremendous, but the results were farcical.

Let me recall the pageant, which was planned as the main attraction for La Semana Alegra, or Week of Joy celebration, which took place traditionally in February. This particular performance was in the early 1950s, and was designed to be a cultural exhibition.

Appointed as pageant director was a woman known as Mme. Irma Labastille. She was large and energetic and had an expanded imagination to match her upholstered, continental-shelf bosom. She had come here from Miami at the request of officials to whom she had been recommended as an expert.

On arrival, feted by local society fixtures, Mme. Labastille made a hurried study of material for the pageant. Her conglomerate knowledge was incorporated with what must have been previous experience in the more classic forms of dance, drama and historical productions. Accent was on mob scenes. She had a Cecil B. deMille penchant, and might have been good at composing banquet scenes for Roman revels.

But Key West adults, being the independent segment as usual, did not respond to the call for participation en masse. Local students were recruited for the casting.

On with the show. More than five hundred spectators turned out at West Martello Tower (now the Garden Center), where bleachers were set up on the grounds. The center stage was in what is now an outdoor display area. The evening began serenely, but the wind velocity continued to increase. Mini-gales kicked up a caper at a minimum of twenty-three miles-per-hour, and havoc resulted!

First, a contrived galleon, which was to furnish offshore background, broke its moorings. Since it was only flimsy scenery, it took off for parts unknown, along with other hunks of impressionistic backdrops—gone with the gusts.

Undaunted, the audience huddled on the board seats, clamping on to caps, hats, capes, stoles, shawls, and mantillas, and the show went on in the best "show biz" tradition. There were some high-lights in the opening setting with a Fountain of Youth structure, complete with two huge goblets and giant sea horses as the central design. Around this creation danced nymphs in filmy garments subject to the whims of the wind. Southern exposure resulted in appreciative whistles from the males in the audience.

Musical background was excellent. A chorus of about fifty vocal-ists was directed by the late Tom Whitley. The singers were accompanied by pianist Millicent Taylor. The sound of the sea and wind blended in with enchanting results, part of the time. Unfortunately the blend was not consistent. Without adequate sound equipment, as the wind velocity increased, voices were carried away in sporadic puffs.

Up on an embankment, sixty high school students chanted the stories of historical sequence with some difficulty, since they held fluttering scripts and flashlights in order to read the overlong lines incorporated into the pageant by the director.

After the prologue, as described, Scene II burst in on the outdoor stage with piercing screams and war whoops, delivered with enthusiasm by more students got up as tribes of early Indians, Calusas versus Caribes. The savages entered into the fierce combat with zest. Outside of football scrimmages, Key West had not seen such riotous frenzy in years.

Scalping action was easy. The wigs of long black braids didn't have to be "lifted" by the warriors. Nearly every one of the fighters flipped and lost his wig as the struggle went on, until there was complete annihilation. All those loose scalps, strewn willy-nilly on the battleground, "slew" the audience.

To make it all the more hilarious, a small band of strangely calm Indians sat on the sidelines and beat their tom-toms. You couldn't "hear them for miles." The drum tones were just barely audible in the noisy melee.

In the sequence, a few Spaniards in helmets and armor appeared on the scene and discovered what was supposedly a pile of bones, aftermath of the tremendous conflict between native tribes. Scarlet banners of Spain and a white one of the Church were planted on the soil. The name Cayo Hueso, Isle of Bones, was pronounced by a black-robed priest. This scene was truly dramatic, with the armor gleaming in the moonlight. But, alas, the effect was marred. The moonlight also reflected with a glitter on the modern eyeglasses worn by many of the explorers.

Pirates were depicted next, landing not like Marines, the situation well in hand, but with careless abandon, rolling in, roistering and guzzling bottles of rum (synthetic, of course). The motley crew (and never was an expression more appropriate) kept taking swigs between bouts of burying a treasure chest, along with a couple of their own men, after flashing displays of earrings, gritted teeth and swordplay. Someone in the audience cracked, "Looks like an overflow delegation from Sloppy Joe's."

Years of the wreckers were marked by a witty sermon delivered by Fr. John Armstrong of St. Paul's Episcopal Church. He portrayed "The Wrecking Parson," who kept his congregation enthralled while he, having spotted a wreck from the elevation of his pulpit, made his way down the aisle to the door, and then put on a dash to his salvage vessel shouting, "Wreck ashore!" At least so goes the legend.

Actors in this part of the pageant were attired in 1825 costumes. One couple arrived in a creaking buckboard drawn by an equally creaky horse. At one point the horse balked and seemed to want to stay in the limelight. There was a little confusion about getting him offstage. He left souvenirs of his appearance.

Ethnic groups fared better with interludes of a rhumba band, a calypso unit, and a choral insert by students from Douglass High School, plus the Key West High School band. These musical treats were esteemed as toppers of the evening.

Ironically, the ballet on the 1935 Labor Day Hurricane proved to be almost as disastrous as the devastation of the Flagler Railroad. A handsome and popular couple portrayed the "Spirits of the Hurricane." They stood high on a fort embankment. The robes they wore were wind-tossed, and the performers were hard put to maintain a semblance of dignity and modesty, not to mention precarious balance. Between classical posturing, the tableaux figures were given to madly clutching their garments with the wind fighting to tear the robes not only asunder, but completely away.

Climax came when a quartet of Navy men sang old sea ditties, including the ancient chantey, "Blow, Blow, Blow the Man Down." The irony of the whole situation was too much and the audience responded with whoops of laughter.

To cap the climax, announcement was made next day that a local physician had been hospitalized with a broken leg. He had aspired to take part in the drama and to advise on action. He had climbed one of the higher battlements at West Martello, surveyed the scene, made a magnificent gesture appropriate to his role of pride, and toppled down a steep embankment.

"Pride cometh before..."–and all that.

NIGHT FLASHER

Key West has always been photogenic, and, through the years, with the help of Larry Rogers at the Chamber of Commerce, it has attracted camera crews from all sorts of publications to shoot background scenes as well as action. We have become accustomed to seeing high fashion models, including Margaux Hemingway, posing for advertising agency work.

Several movies have been filmed here; more of that angle will be forthcoming in a later chapter. For the present, here's a sidelight of one mad adventure involving an ace photographer who came here in the early 1950s for *Life Magazine*.

The chief photographer, George Leavens, was then married to Marion Light, now familiar to Key Westers as Marion Stevens. His main job was to take a series of pictures to go with a *Life* article dedicated to what were then new sonar methods of detecting submarines. At that time, in the 1951–1953 period or thereabouts, experimentation was being conducted in anti-submarine warfare, coordinating subs, surface craft, planes and helicopters. Technical details were supposed to be very "hush-hush."

The system being explored encompassed a small contingent of British Royal Air Force and Royal Navy fliers stationed here in Key West.

Leavens, who came from Australia to America, decided to add extracurricular photography just for a sidelight. He dropped in at the *Key West Citizen* to look into feature possibilities of the night club beat in the area.

Since I had recently been an entertainment editor for the *Miami Daily News*, and was acquainted with the island's taverns, pubs, and so-called nightclubs, I had been recommended as guide and source of information of after-dark action. I submitted a list of sites which Leavens might find interesting.

George already had ventured entry at the Habana Madrid and the Mardi Gras, two of the most famous (or infamous) "joints," several of the Duval Street bars, and numerous waterfront haunts. But he wanted to sample a few more places on his last night here.

Sloppy Joe's, corner of Duval and Greene Streets, was much like it is today: huge bar and canopy of parachutes. But back then there was a small dance floor where special acts were performed. On this particular evening a bit of exotica/erotica called the Mystery Dancer was billed, so that was our first port of call.

I had to get permission from the Sloppy Joe's manager for George to take photos, and did so with ease when the proprietor was told that his establishment might be part of a *Life Magazine* layout. We traipsed into Sloppy Joe's with enthusiasm and a camera and light paraphernalia. I guarded what George wasn't setting up when we seated ourselves on stools barside to await the appearance of the star performer. I assumed, of course, that she had been given the magic password—*Life Magazine.*

The overhead lights dimmed, a taped recording of "Caravan" vibrated in the barroom, and from the nether regions of the ladies' rest room there emerged a mysterious figure completely swathed, head to toe, in black gauzy veiling.

Gyrating, slowly at first, to the desert rhythm, the dancer began hootchie-kootchie movements with swirls and twirls, bumps and grinds, but with a difference. She threw a little light on the subject. She held a flashlight in one hand under the enveloping black veil. The big cylinder was capped with red glass at one end and green at the other terminal.

As the dancer's footwork progressed, she aimed the light, in alternate stop and go signals, to encircle parts of her anatomy. Since she wore a minimum set of breast pasties and only a heart-shaped shield over her…most strategic zone, the roving light was quite illuminating.

Intrepid George decided to try a from-the-floor angle. He slid out on the dance floor, lay face up and took aim.

Now this lensman was known for great exploits such as taking underwater shots of sharks on the Great Barrier Reef off Australia. He was usually a wary photographer. But he was unprepared for this event. The writhing dancer paused, then advanced on little cat feet. She screamed epithets and began to kick the prostrate George. He was so busy trying to protect his equipment—the camera, that is—that he took several hefty foot blows before he stood up. The shrieked curses were encouraged by all the bar hounds who howled with laughter.

The manager finally interfered, and while George was dusting himself off I attempted to mollify the "Mystery Dancer." But she stalked off indignantly, still encased in the black shroud disguise.

I found out later that she was the wife of a Navy man and was "moonlighting" as a novelty dancer. Important magazine or no, she resented any intrusion or publicity.

Intrepid George was determined to get a night-bird's eye view. We left amidst hoots and bleats from the customers and went down Duval Street to the somewhat lurid old Tropics to pay our respects (if you'll pardon the term in this connection).

The Tropics was located at the corner of Duval and Angela Streets where the distinguished Lowell C. Restaurant was later located. But in the bad old days, it was the hangout for militant military—Marines, Navy, and a few Coast Guardsmen, as well as some local rowdies. The Army wasn't stationed on the Keys at that time. Some residents visited the Tropics "just for kicks." The band was good, though most of the entertainment consisted of second rate singers, third rate comedians, and à fourth rate string of G-stringed girlies.

We wandered in and found a table fairly close to the stage. The five-piece group of musicians played "A Pretty Girl is Like a Melody" with lassitude, except for cymbal crashes and a drum riff. A gum-chewing brassy blond appeared for the first "take-off."

George glanced around and seemed discouraged. "Same old stuff. All blah! No real action," he said.

And no sooner were the words out of his mouth when he was belied. Over in a corner where a bunch of Navy men jammed a

table near another crowded with stalwarts of the U.S. Marine Corps, there began a row, at first with verbal thrusts, then an exchange of follow up punches. Bottle-throwing added to the stir, which rapidly whipped into a real mix-master's brouhaha. The slugfest spread and developed into the violence of a near-riot in seconds.

I prepared to duck under the table, because glasses were flying through the air and chairs were being tossed. But George grinned in happy anticipation, hoisted his camera and took aim.

He may have taken a few shots, but not more than that, when a bouncer grabbed his arm. "None of that, Bubba! We don't want no pictures. Just get out," the hulking guard ordered.

In the distance came the wail of sirens and squad cars. "Please, let's go," I pleaded. With a gesture of contempt, George once again collected the cameras. As we jostled our way to the exit, we met the first arrival of the Shore Patrol wading inside to break up the fracas.

We finally found a taxi and I relaxed, murmuring, "No action, eh?" George laughed. "Maybe I got a few worthwhile shots, but I doubt it."

I suggested we had better try for a more peaceful slice of night life. He agreed. We went to the Casa Marina Hotel, where sedate social dancing was the order of the evening.

The moonlit patio, just off the Bird Cage Lounge, was rimmed with local people. The music was furnished by an excellent Latin American band. Leavens executed a skillful rhumba and then cast about for a photo sequence.

We were relaxing with cool drinks when up came a Royal Air Force officer with whom I was acquainted. I introduced Leavens to him and smiled in anticipation of a pleasant chat.

But the RAFer stiffened and asked, "Are you one of the chaps with the *Life Magazine* crew?"

George, still standing after introductions, so identified himself.

"Well, sir," intoned the RAF officer, "you have invaded what was supposed to be a military secret. You are little more than a spy!" He turned abruptly and left us. I was flabbergasted. George was indignant. We left the otherwise placid setting. George vetoed any further forays into life on the night set.

Just a few weeks later *Life Magazine* came out with a front page cover showing a plane towing a sonar sub-detecting instrument in the ocean on anti-submarine maneuvers. Snorted the British, "Top secret. hush-hush. my arse! You Americans allowed a national magazine to come out with the whole thing!"

PARTY LINE – ONE

Key West enjoys an enduring reputation of being a party town, although the extreme liveliness has abated somewhat since the departure from the island of various military contingents.

However, the town still exhibits animated festivities, especially in the winter season on weekends.

There was a time when even mid-week nights were given over to what was known as "wing-dings," "bashes," and "whoop-de-dos," and the party line was a-tingle, almost continuously, with costume parties.

One party of yesteryear was based on the Bridey Murphy motif of reincarnation. All of the guests devoted their costumes to what they thought they might have been in past centuries. Favorite characters of novels, historical figures throughout the ages, subjects related to famous artists and paintings inspired merrymaking.

One artists' gathering brought out Richard Brooks as "Self Portrait." He simply hung a picture frame around his head and face.

The Navy, markedly the submarine divisions, went in for elaborate events and extravaganzas, with participants dressed up according to designated themes. Local naval retirees, like Roy and Barbara Anderson and Marge and Bill Westray, were always active in the party-show events at Fort Taylor.

I remember one such celebration in which a bevy of submariners arrived in regalia appropriate to the theme, "Neptune's Court," with even a mermaid in a portable bathtub luring landlubbers.

Largely a civilian affair, although hosted by the Navy's Barbara and Walter Schlech, it was a "Come As Your Favorite Song" occasion. The winner was a daring interpretation of a prevalent jukebox tune, "The Half-Fast Waltz." One of the Royal Air Force officers, stationed here with Helicopter Squadron One, swaggered boldly around with one half of his trousers hacked off in the rear, permitting a southern exposure in keeping with the song title when pronounced on the double. Try it verbally.

"Toga parties" swept campuses across the country after the movie *Animal House* was released to delighted audiences. While I was viewing the cinema version of this fraternity house toga party, the vivid recollection of a Roman Holiday Rites of Spring fete, celebrated in May of 1952, surged back in memory.

58

The "When-in-Rome" festival was held in honor of a couple from New York City, house guests of Jeanne Porter Kirk, who is now Mrs. Art Poirier of San Francisco. She is the daughter of the late "Miss Jessie," Mrs. E.L. Newton of Key West.

The fanciful event took place in my apartment at 616 Duval Street, upstairs over what was then the Southernmost Flower and Gift Shop. There was a spacious former dance studio in the second story that accommodated partygoers, as well as space downstairs. The entire area was arranged in a Roman-style scene with household gods of Lares and Penates, a temple altar, and a pool with a phallic symbol of Pompeian design.

All illumination was by votive candlelight inside and torchlight outside. There were no couches on which to loll, but pallets and cushions lined the walls, and a couple of noble Roman thrones were set up. Modern note was carried out in the bar and a buffet. Decorations of flower, palm fronds, and leafy bowers prevailed throughout the setting.

Guests arrived in costumes of considerably more variety and ingenuity than just draped bed sheets, although those, too, were converted into Roman garments. Nobles and royalty wore a touch of purple. Laurel wreaths (sapodilla and oleander were reasonable substitutes) adorned the males. Scantily clad handmaidens and slaves, a fugitive from a Roman galley ship, a brace of gladiators in foil armor, and a chariot driver with a whip were represented.

Joe Hurka, a Key West teacher posing as Marc Antony, came to praise Caesar, and found half a dozen of them! Exotic priestesses, a Phonetical Phoenician trader, a Roman Athlete Afoot, were part of the throng, plus Nero, who had no violin, but played a flute.

Costume prize was awarded the most unique pair. Visiting Visigoths, barbarians who invaded Rome, were clad in animal skis, mostly fake, but with a couple of moth-eaten raccoon pelts in their ensemble. The lady barbarian, DeeDee Agricola, was arrayed in sack cloth with a real hambone twisted through her primitive topknot. One rugged individual was disguised as a Roman candle.

As for me, I was draped as Herod's infamous daughter, in seven flowing veils, and bore a platter with two miniature chamber pots on it. The Navy expression "the head" was utilized, and my placard proclaimed "Two Heads Are Better Than One."

After a midnight curfew, the Romans went a-roamin' in the gloamin', scattering to the traditional Seven Hills of the city–in this case, beyond Solares Hill–with a Roman bathos finale. One group decided to go swimming at the Sun and Sands Beach Club, even though it was closed at that late hour and did not permit swimming after dark. The cavorters in the water abandoned suits after submerging and tossed swim gear up along the shore.

But somebody notified the police, and a patrol car approached the site, sirens going full blast. This, of course, alerted the swimmers. One of them who was still clad rushed to the edge of the beach and tossed bathing suits willy-nilly into the water. When the cops summoned the culprits ashore, every one of them had managed to put on haphazard covering, ill-assorted though it was.

The police, usually tolerant, simply warned the chastened swimmers to disperse.

The second unit of aftermath celebrants, of which I was one, piled into a car–eight of us–and drove to a deserted stretch of Boca Chica beach. There we entered the shallow water, splashed about, disporting with abandon, and finally abandoned our swimsuits, throwing them up on the sand.

All went swimmingly, so to speak, until an automobile loaded with sailors pulled up and focussed headlights on the water shore line, pinning our party in the glare.

We all crouched in the water until mosquito hordes attacked. So we skinny-dippers decided to risk a dash for our car, pausing only to scoop up swim attire, and drove off. There was a mad scramble as the passengers got into suits as we departed.

Now for the denouement. As a result of the Roman rites of spring and fertility, the visitors from New York married upon return to the big city, and nine months to the day after the festivity, twins were born to them.

I understood later that the babies were girls, and so were not named Romulus and Remus.

THE NIGHT PEOPLE

A fine raconteur, the late Earle Saunders Johnson. He owned and lived in the Oldest House, now a Duval Street museum, and used to regale listeners at parties around town and at his home with stories about Key West. He was born here and resided for some of his boyhood years in Key West before moving to New England, where he was educated. He kept returning to the island for long stays and eventually came back here to set up his permanent residence. He knew the Old Rock intimately.

Earle loved to shock audiences and often exaggerated his stories, but the essence of truth was always there. For example, he used to say, "You know my father was electrocuted," and of course strangers always wondered what sort of crime had been involved. Earle would explain that the electrocution was an accident when his father came in contact with a live wire while on the job as a linesman. I was fully aware that in his story-telling Earle indulged his love of creating interesting topics of conversation, and sometimes did so just for sensationalism. So when he talked about the "hidden colony of lepers on the island," I thought he was up to his old attention-getting tricks.

Earle claimed that, during daytime hours, a large group of native Conchs were secreted in out-of-the-way houses on obscure lanes and byways of Key West. They ventured out of concealment only under cover of darkness. Said he, "They hide from the sight of anybody outside of their immediate family circles because they suffer from leprosy. They are afraid they will be shipped off to the leper headquarters in Carville, Louisiana, where there is a hospital isolation treatment center for lepers."

Earle went on to divulge that most of the unfortunate victims of the dread disease were related and very clannish. Their kin concealed them from the public eye, not only because of appearances, for many of them had reached conditions of deformity, but because there were strong bonds of family loyalties and affection. Nobody wanted to have relatives separated from them and sent off to the hospital, even though treatment was available there. In fact, most of the families accepted leprosy as a turn of fate, and believed that there was no cure or sure treatment.

"If you should wander into the back sections of our movie balconies late at night," Earle advised, "you might spot some of the 'Night People.' Some have disfigured faces and some are crippled and have lost fingers, toes and even limbs. They attend the second shows, creeping in late, after the regular patrons are seated, and creeping out again after the crowds have left the theaters."

I asked how he knew all this. He replied that he had witnessed the off-hour comings and goings and that he personally knew some of the afflicted. He added that he hadn't reported the incidents to health authorities for several reasons. First of all he felt sorry for the people involved and realized the emotional stress. Besides, the "Night People" were not in close contact with the general public and weren't harmful. He also hinted that the conditions were known to local authorities but that the situation remained secret so as not to create bad publicity for the community.

"The Navy might pull out. People might panic," Earle reasoned, "if they knew what was going on."

He contended that Hansen's Disease, the preferred medical term for leprosy, was not as contagious as smallpox, for example, and could not be acquired easily, and only through prolonged physical contact. "If the families want to risk this, then it's up to them," he said. "As long as the persons who have the disease are isolated from the rest of the community, why stir up trouble?"

His attitude of laissez-faire is a Key West characteristic and has been for years. I talked only recently to several Key Westers, and all of them concurred in the opinion that it was up to the individual families to decide what to do about members who had developed the sickness. One woman, who was just a child when she learned that a relative of hers by marriage was a leper, informed me that the unfortunate man was simply "put in a back room at his house and kept there. Eventually he died."

Another lady said, "When we first came to Key West back in the 1930s, there were quite a few cases in town and lots of people know about it. Folks just kept their mouths shut because they were afraid the afflicted would be separated from their loved ones and sent off to Louisiana."

There was only meager understanding of Hansen's Disease back in the old days. And there was a profound stigma attached to "HD," as leprosy is often designated. Years of study and research have brought a better understanding of the problem. But in the days when fear and misunderstanding of the condition was prevalent, treatment was neglected and, in Key West, the leprosy spread.

What brought the revelation of truth about leprosy on the island,

and incidentally, confirmation of Earle Johnson's stories, was the accidental discovery in 1953-54 of the facts by a *Key West Citizen* reporter, Pat Wood. She covered the Public Health Service beat and happened to stumble on a disturbing report made by a Public Health employee, a school nurse. The nurse had served in the South Pacific with the Armed Forces during World War II and was familiar with lepers and indications of Hansen's Disease.

During a routine examination of school children, she found that one child had symptoms of early leprosy. The health department began investigating. In fact, Naval authorities, with far-reaching officialdom, insisted on a thorough tracking of cases. They threatened to pull out of the Key West area unless this was done.

The medical detective work was kept secret. Not one word of the process was printed in the newspapers, locally or in Miami. The project was persistently pursued and led to the discovery that fifteen or more persons in the same neighborhood and family unit were potential patients, either with advanced cases or just the start of Hansen's Disease. As the investigation advanced, thirty-three cases of leprosy were uncovered, a larger number than anywhere in the United States outside of the hospital for lepers at Carville, Louisiana.

Emergency measures were applied at once. Local treatment for the milder cases was proscribed. The more advanced patients were treated in isolated groups and some were transferred, at least temporarily, to Carville. Gradual, elimination of the problem took place, and in time the undercover talk died down except for vague rumors and usual juicy background gossip.

Then on August 31, 1959, some five years after the major campaign to rid the area of leprosy, another case cropped up. This time there was no concealment since the matter was connected with a crime. The case became common knowledge and drew grandstand play in all the media.

The Clerk of the Criminal Court, Harry Dongo, 51, was arrested and charged with embezzlement, allegedly for padding the payroll for jurors. He was placed in the county jail September 1, 1959, under $5,000 bond. But on October 14, six weeks after he was first apprehended, Dongo was re-arrested. A $10,000 bond was set.

Back in jail Dongo was examined by a physician who exclaimed, "You can't keep this man imprisoned! He has leprosy and must be sent off to Carville for immediate treatment. There is a penal division connected with the hospital."

At first Dongo had pleaded "not guilty by reason of insanity" through his attorney, J.Y. Porter. The Criminal Court Judge was the late Thomas A. Caro, with whom Dongo had been associated in legal processes for years. A plea for mercy, on account of Dongo's health, was made by attorney Porter. Medical evidence was given by County Health Officer Dr. J.L. Wardlow, who had diagnosed Dongo's condition as "tubercular leprosy," which is difficult to determine.

On November 19, 1959, after Dongo's plea was changed to guilty, Judge Caro handed down what was termed "a complicated sentence." His verdict: Dongo was sentenced to serve six to ten years in the state prison on the first count. But this was suspended on condition that the defendant be immediately placed in a hospital, "for suspected leprosy." Judge Caro pronounced the prison sentence suspended while Dongo was placed in the Carville Center for treatment for his affliction.

"But if you leave for any reason," said Caro, "you will be required to serve the prison sentence in a penitentiary." Within 24 hours, Dongo was to be on his way to Louisiana, or at least sent back to the county jail to await transfer.

State officials were happy with the judge's decision, admitting that they would not like to have Dongo in prison where he would have to be isolated due to possible infection of other prisoners. A constable was appointed. The next day, November 20, 1959, Harry Dongo was escorted to Carville.

Louis Carbonell told of having the Clerk of Criminal Court office thoroughly fumigated before he moved in. "I wasn't taking any chances," he said. "All I found in the office to indicate that Harry was distressed was a whole batch of empty liquor bottles. And who could blame him for a drinking problem under the circumstances? He realized what his trouble was."

I was the *Citizen* reporter on the courthouse beat for a long time, and in the early 1950s spent time with Dongo every day after the morning sessions in Caro's court. We would go over the facts as to charge and sentence, fines, and so on. I checked the records with him at my side and carefully took down notes. While in close proximity to Harry, I never suspected his disease.

I had noticed that he had a reddish, scaly nose, but I thought it was due to heavy drinking when off duty. I attributed the white areas I saw on his hands to a natural condition of the skin, and thought the brown spots had been caused by a liver condition. Actually, it must have been the other way around. His natural skin color was brown, and the white parts must have been the start of leprosy lesions.

Dongo was always cooperative and patient with me in getting material for the *Citizen*. When he was discovered to have falsified jury records, I felt sorry for him. When the revelation came of his physical condition, I thought it tragic.

I saw him once more about eight or nine years after his sentence in the fall of 1959. He was sitting on a bench on a corner of Duval Street and called to me. He looked much better than he had before he left, and we shook hands. I sat beside him, and he told me of existence at Carville. He said that treatment had at least brought about temporary remission of his disease. "They let me come here for a visit, but I have to go back and continue treatment," he said. A little wistfully he added, "At least down there I'm not avoided, and I have friends who aren't afraid of me."

Louis Carbonell corresponded with Dongo through the years, and believed that the one-time return to Key West was the only time Dongo had legally been permitted to leave the hospital. Carbonell also said that Harry Dongo died in Carville in the late 1970s.

There are new treatments for leprosy. There are two distinct kinds: tubercular leprosy, which is what Harry Dongo had, and a more severe form caused by mycobacterium leprae bacillus, in which destruction of peripheral nerves leads to characteristic loss of sensation in the afflicted parts. This loss of sensation, together with progressive tissue degeneration, if left untreated, may result in deformity of the extremities: the nose, hands, feet, and even limbs, as well as the testes, and sometimes the eyes. This is because when the germ invades, it seeks the cooler portions of the body and the mucous membranes.

There is a great deal more to the technical description of Hansen's Disease, and pertinent facts concerning latest theories and the drugs being used. Isolation, at least temporary isolation, and the taking of medicines (including Dapsone and other drugs) are necessary for control and helpful therapy.

Leprosy is now believed to be carried by a virus through the upper respiratory system and not through skin contact. So there should be less trembling fear of casual contact with those who have Hansen's Disease. Modern methods arrest the affliction if applied in early stages. Precautions are taken, of course, and an important one is to separate newborn babies from leprous parents and a potentially dangerous environment. This preventive measure was not observed in earlier, less informed years, contributing to the large number of cases of leprosy in Key West (and elsewhere).

Some ninety percent of the people in the world are immune or not susceptible to leprosy. Hansen's Disease is, however, indigenous to tropical and sub-tropical regions, including the Caribbean area and states bordering the Gulf of Mexico. It is developed in California and Hawaii and throughout the South Pacific regions.

In the United States—especially in Florida—surveillance and improved public health services, plus expanded medical knowledge, are keeping HD under control.

DOWN THE HATCH

The USS *Sea Dog* (S 401), a Key West-based submarine, was skippered by Cmdr. James B. Elliott, Jr. He was justifiably proud of the *Sea Dog* softball team, but the sports editor of the *Key West Citizen*, Jim Cobb, was too busy to attend Navy inter-ship games played on the Naval Station recreation field. The baseball games in 1952 were enthusiastic events attended by entire families, not only Navy rooters, but lots of civilians and townspeople as supporters. Games were exciting and fun to watch. I've forgotten how it came about that I was maneuvered into covering a game between the USS *Sea Dog* and the USS *Sea Poacher*.

Cmdr. Elliott and his wife, Gina, called for me at 6 P.M. one evening in September. Jimmy Elliott III, nine years old, was bat boy for the *Sea Dog*. His brother, John, who was "almost five," also wore a blue and white uniform with the *Sea Dog* emblem—a fish with the head of a bulldog—on the shirt. Young John had on a bright red cap, so his mother could spot him from a distance. Intrepid John had a habit of emulating his big brother in picking up bats. The trouble was John didn't care what team it was for which he picked up the bats, so a close surveillance had to be maintained.

On arrival at the field, I apologized for not being a regular sports writer and admitted I would be a little hazy on the play-by-play description. The team manager, Navy Chief Harold Smith, accepted the substitution with a shrug and a smile.

We climbed into the bleachers agilely, if not gracefully, and I was introduced to the wives and children of the players. The mothers and moppets who filled the stand prepared to yell for the Sea Dog Nine. They even brought throat lozenges!

The Sea Dogs were breaking in natty new uniforms that game. Never say that uniforms make the team. But they certainly help. The *Sea Poacher* opposition appeared in nondescript outfits, fatigue pants, and scruffy shirts. A few wore red caps. They also had an indifferent spirit. With tenacity and consistent skill, apropos of the quickness of the fish-and-bulldog determination of the emblem, the *Sea Dog* players won, 33-10.

As a result of my write-up of the game, I was invited to have lunch aboard the submarine three days afterward. It was an unforgettable experience.

I accepted with optimistic alacrity. Alas, there were no etiquette manuals on eating aboard a submarine, so I had to make do with a few suggestions from people who gave me some fine details. They weren't fine or detailed enough!

First of all, there was the problem of how to dress. I knew a tight skirt would be confining. So I selected a plain cotton dress with a full loose skirt. Remember, this was back in the 1950s, and only the very young wore the jeans which have since become fashionable.

It's too bad that I wasn't given proper advice, including carrying a special gadget for loosening skirt hems which catch and hook on unexpected projections inside a submarine hatch.

There also should have been X-ray glasses to wear, so that it would be possible for me to see through dress material.

A few additional forewarnings should be given to prospective lady visitors to submarines who aren't young and supple and have not had acrobatic training. It would be wise to do some setting up exercises in advance, chiefly deep-knee bends and ladder climbing. It also would facilitate sub expeditions to practice hanging on a bar (not the honky-tonk variety) and doing walking-on-air exercises.

Perhaps, some day, there will be metal poles in subs, the kind they have in fire stations, to slide down, and a hoist to yank a guest from the interior to the deck. But back then you just took a desperate gulp of air and made a silent toast: "Down the Hatch!"

Capt. Elliott explained that a submarine was no place for dignified entrances or exits. How right he was.

I started down a perpendicular ladder through a circular opening into the depths of the *Sea Dog*. Facing the ladder, I stepped down one rung, then two, and made it to three. I was reaching for the fourth rung of the steep ladder when a breeze from the interior of the sub came whooping up and blew my skirt right in front of my face. The hem caught on a metal protuberance above my head, and there I hung suspended, one foot dangling, trying to find purchase on the next rung.

"Unhook your skirt," came the command from above. But I was afraid to let go of my hold on the sides of the ladder to do so, and I couldn't see through the skirt which ballooned up over my head, obscuring the caught-upon obstacle.

I could hear a muttered consultation from the deck. Then a sailor was lowered, head first, to unsnag me. He did this by hanging upside down, held by his ankles, then was hoisted back up the hatch to the deck. To keep the billowing skirt from catching again, I snatched at it with my teeth and gripped it there so that I could at least peer about me. I again began the perilous descent.

Capt. Elliott called down to crewmen below, "Secure eyes!" Afterward I found out that meant for all below-deck crewman to face the hull away from me and the ladder on which I was slowly inching down into the interior.

I finally stepped off the last rung and sighed with relief. I don't know how the men below managed to suppress laughter, but they did.

The ordeal didn't end then. Every other step toward the wardroom, where luncheon was to be served, involved ducking my head. Finally, we were seated at the officer's mess table. I looked at my guest card and found I had been made an honorary member of the *Sea Dog's* softball team.

The chef on the *Sea Dog* was Enrique Cruz, from Guam, the man who pitched for the softball nine. He pitched in the galley too, right over the hot plate, and produced a gourmet repast.

Another bit of advice to luncheon guests aboard submarines: don't eat breakfast that day. When "lunch" was served it was a full-sized, full-course meal, more like a dinner, with leafy salad, tangy dressing, buttered corn on the cob, sauteed mushrooms, french fried potatoes and broiled steak. The dessert was ice-cream with chocolate sauce, followed by coffee. I can vouch for the saying, "The Marines get the glory, the Army (infantry) get the marching, and the Navy gets the chow."

The visit below deck ended, and I made a final panting (and I mean that) ascent to upper strata. But I retained touches of claustrophobia.

The USS *Sea Dog's* achievements weren't confined to athletic endeavors. Some time later, the submarine, on a maneuver up the coast, rescued a straying Navy blimp and towed it into port. The feat gained national acclaim and international headlines. When the submarine returned to Key West, it was tendered a razzle-dazzle reception. Once again I was invited to attend a special coffee reception aboard the submarine. But this time I adamantly refused to go down a hatch. I sipped my coffee safely on the nice level deck.

I suspect that the officers and crew were relieved at not having to repeat escorting me below.

TWELVE MILE

In the Spring of 1953, a movie first known as *Twelve Mile Reef,* and later as *Beneath the Twelve Mile Reef* (doubtless due to aroused interest in undersea movies), was filmed here. Most of the action took place on land. A few scenes were shot at Tarpon Springs and some in Florida Keys waters, but Key West had the major role.

Jeff Knight, who headed the Florida State Employment office in Key West then, smilingly reported that more than one hundred people streamed into his office without advance publicity. Extras got $10 a day, and if a speaking part was assigned the salary went up to $70 a day. Knight said it was the first time a movie company had asked the employment office for aid in rounding up authentic waterfront characters, fishermen and shrimpers.

Twentieth Century Fox selected seventy-five Key West dwellers for roles, among them Jack Burke, then editor of the Navy publication *The Outpost.* Jack had to give up his typewriter and his razor for the duration of his acting assignment as a burly waterfront brawler. The plot was about the one-time feuding between Conchs and Greek sponge fishermen.

The chief Greek spongers were played by J. Carrol Nash, Robert Wagner and Gilbert Roland. There was one special scene that took place in Duffy's Tavern, where Delmonico's is now on Duval Street. The tavern atmosphere was certainly authentic, and the row that was staged when the Greeks and the Conchs mixed it up looked as if it were, too. At that time, there was a much-favored jukebox song, *One Meat Ball,* and it was taken up as a chant by the extras when not before the camera. The original ditty went, "One meat ball, one meat ball, you don't get any bread with one meat ball." The people in the tavern sequence changed this to "Not one meat ball and no spaghetti at all," since plates heaped with spaghetti were placed on the tables, but nobody could actually eat the food because the exact setting had to be maintained due to re-takes.

The younger generation favored Robert Wagner, Peter Graves, and Terry Moore, but Key West women of all ages clamored for autographs of Gilbert Roland, last of the Great Latin Lovers School. He was still handsome and dashing, and moved with romantic swagger.

During a scene played in front of the Florida First National Bank,

70

the street surfaces near the corner of Duval and Front, had to be continuously wetted down by a hose attached to the corner hydrant. The work was supervised by the fire department. There had been a water shortage during this period, and someone shouted, "There goes my shower bath for tonight!"

However, everyone–spectators, police, firemen and the film makers, including the cast–grooved in carnival mood. When the scene at the bank was finished, after about an hour and a half, Gilbert Roland whipped a red bandana from his hip pocket, flourished it like a miniature bullfighter's cape, and Wagner charged at him with his index fingers pointed alongside his dark curly head imitating a horned bull.

Roland was always gallant, and courteous to the crowds, especially to ladies. I saw him lose his aplomb only once during all those weeks on location. He gave a special Spanish dinner at Ramonin's, a restaurant situated on Duval where Antonio's is at present. The movie crew, cast, press and special guests from townspeople ranks were invited. The restaurant was not open to the public, but it was not inconvenient for regular diners, for the evening chosen was on the regular closing day.

Unfortunately, a brash young man managed to crash the gathering by posing as a waiter. He entered the dining room, marched up to Roland, and demanded an autograph right in the middle of the main course. Roland, tall and stalwart, rose majestically and boomed, "Do I break into your house at dinner time and bother you? Now go at once or I'll throw you out personally. If you care to wait a couple of hours outside, I'll give you an autograph when we have finished eating."

The guests applauded and the invader retreated.

One slack afternoon when Roland was not needed for a shooting session, he invited me to go swimming in the lagoon protected by wire just off the pier that extended into the sea at the Casa Marina. He wasn't too pleased with the enclosed swimming area, but later admitted it was a necessary safety measure. After getting out of the barricaded swimming section we strolled to the edge of the pier and found Dr. Ralph Herz straining to bring in some denizen of the deep which was bending the fishing pole.

Actor Roland took over for a few minutes until Dr. Herz restored circulation to his cramped hands. The fish leaped up. It was a four-foot barracuda! The line snapped finally and it sped off. Roland cracked, "I thought barracuda hung around bars." Barracuda was the nickname for B-girls in the 1950s.

Back at the hotel, we ran into Harry Carey, Jr., and Richard Boone of the cast, and were invited to join them in the Bird Cage Lounge to "have a belt." So I learned that a belt was not something to hold up trousers, but a California expression for having a drink.

Bob Youmans, a lawyer who had been working as a stand-in for Roland and had had to have his blond hair dyed black, appeared to announce that the next day he would be back to being fair-haired again, since he was switching to a stand-in for blond Peter Graves. When he left he waved airily and cracked, "See you in the beauty parlor!" You could have blown me over with a hair-dryer. Anyway, the *Citizen* ran a picture of Youmans getting his hair coloring, and the caption read "Local Boy Fakes Good."

Dick Boone, now deceased, enjoyed a reunion with his erstwhile

fellow gunner bomb diver in the Navy, Eddie Irwin, who had become Aviation Ordinance Chief with the AUW School in Key West. When Boone was out of earshot, Irwin confided, "Dick is too modest. Bet you don't know, and he won't tell you, but he had a terrific World War II record."

Certainly Boone had diversified traits. He talked to a drama class at the Key West High School and made a personal appearance at the San Carlos Theater with Terry Moore. He helped supervise the crowds at the A&B Lobster House docks during a night filming in which a sponge boat was set afire, and there was some danger involved. He was a no-nonsense career man, but possessed a bizarre sense of humor which showed up once at Logun's Lobster House, where he had been dining frequently.

Every evening a local girl, who had evidently wished to attract his attention, paraded by his table, thrusting out her chest to display ample frontage. Boone eyed her in appreciation, along with colleagues, but made no comment.

But one night, after about ten days of this bosom boom-boom exhibition, Boone turned to his boon companions and remarked, "I am going to teach Miss Teaser a lesson." When the girl approached promenading pouter-pigeon style, Boone jumped up and ripped open her blouse-topped dress. Surprised, if not shocked, the girl squealed. After all, her falsies were revealed.

Boone said, "I just wanted to see if they were real." He handed her a fifty-dollar bill, and, as far as I know, the incident was closed along with the torn garment.

The company from 20th Century Fox, which arrived in March, was still around in late spring, except for Gilbert Roland, who departed May 19. He left a shirt behind in the aura of good will. Everyone knows the expression, "He's the kind of guy who will give you the shirt off his back." There was more than a mere verbal declaration in this case. At a swank party, a charming woman admired Roland's shirt. He stripped it off, bowed, and presented the garment to the admirer saying, "The shirt is yours, my lady."

When asked about his courtly gesture, Gilbert Roland, who is of Mexican extraction, explained, "It's an old Spanish custom."

In the long list of numerous movie productions made here, on both small and large scales, the *Twelve Mile Reef* film set a record for community participation, along with *The Rose Tattoo*. Both are well recollected by Key Westers who hope for continued cinema industry.

ALL THE MUMMIES AREN'T IN EGYPT

The small island of Key West provides many strange tales, but one of the most bizarre is that of Karl Tanzler, alias Count von Cosel, a German-born pseudo-scientist who kept the corpse of a young Key West girl as his beloved for nearly nine years.

Scores of versions of the macabre happening have appeared in print. I not only read all the material I could find concerning the subject over a period of several years, but I personally interviewed local people who had first hand information about the case.

The exact date that Von Cosel moved to Key West has never been established, but it was some time during the late 1920s or early 1930s. In any case, Von Cosel learned radiology, and had gotten a job as an X-ray technician at the old Marine Hospital.

Physically, Von Cosel fitted the popular conception of a distinguished man of science. He was rather small in build, but he carried himself with dignity and had an air of Old World courtesy. He wore "doctorish" white suits most of the time, although he occasionally donned suits of black alpaca. He also sported an imperial beard.

Von Cosel was 62 years old when Elena was admitted to the Marine Hospital for an examination of her lungs.

Elena Mesa, nee Hoyos, was born July 31, 1909. As a young girl and teenager she was a real beauty, a girl who was popular and who was often photographed. When she was seventeen, she married Louis Mesa. She suffered a miscarriage and returned to the Hoyos family after a separation from Mesa. When she was nineteen, she became a terminal tuberculosis patient.

Nevertheless, Elena was still a lovely girl. She had great dark eyes, long luxuriant black curls, classic Latin features and a slim figure. As soon as she entered the hospital, the aging Von Cosel was captivated by her looks and charm. Indeed, he was so smitten he claimed that she was his "dream girl" come alive, the young woman of whom he had had visions since his boyhood. He declared that he had loved her in the past and that she had once appeared to him while he was admiring statues in another country long ago.

"I saw her, the image of the love I had painted when I was a lad. I talked to her and serenaded her on the organ when we were united again in Austria. When I met her once more at the hospital in Key West, I knew she was the spirit of my dreams and that at last I had found her."

The dying girl, however, spurned Von Cosel as a suitor when he asked her to marry him. He refused to accept her decision. He promised that, even if she died, he would continue treating her by the methods through which he hoped to rebuild her physical condition.

By playing on the ignorance of Elena's parents, Von Cosel convinced them that he could restore Elena's health if they permitted him to treat her with special radiation therapy and injections. This extra treatment was to be carried out at her home.

Von Cosel, who claimed that he was an engineer, a scientist, and a medical expert, as well as an artist, sculptor, musician and potter, said he had built a "high voltage transmitter," which he attached to apparatus installed in the girl's bedroom at her home. In addition to the electrical machinery that he constructed for her, Tanzler-von Cosel, according to later testimony, dissolved gold to put in Elena's drinking water. He brought food to tempt her appetite, and to supplement the diet of her relatives.

It was said that the Hoyos family at first resisted the "devil machine," as they named the electrical rig which the bogus count set up. But they allowed its use in the vain hope that it would help the dying girl. Nevertheless, despite Von Cosel's efforts, Elena had to be returned to the Marine Hospital at various intervals for further examinations by Dr. Harry Galey and a Dr. Lombard.

Although Von Cosel persisted in his advances, Elena refused his proposal of marriage and spurned any physical contact. She did, however, accept financial aid for part of the household expenditures, such as furniture bought on the installment plan. Because Key West was in the doldrums of the Great Depression, the economic support was appreciated by the poor family. In gratitude for "curing" her of an illness, Elena's mother gave the aging benefactor a swath of Elena's luxuriant long tresses which had been cut off a year previously. This turned out to be the source of the hair used to form a wig for the deceased in later days.

As Elena gradually declined in tubercular condition, her admirer persisted in his attentions. He continued to watch over her from the spring of 1930 through the autumn of 1931.

Unfortunately, contradictory and tangled accounts of the life of Tanzler-von Cosel complicate records. Self-declarations varied. Official investigations by psychiatric authorities confirm that the "imposter" was born in Dresden, Germany, about 1869-70, but not of nobility. He had an ordinary education in the public schools of

Germany before he drifted to various parts of the world. He was bright, and in some respects brilliant, with a vibrant curiosity for knowledge. He also was a mystic.

The labyrinth of information on the background of Tanzler included the following claims, some verified, and some simply fantasy, expanded in his "autobiography." In this, Tanzler-von Cosel described his childhood in a castle where he was haunted by a ghost and by visions of boyhood love embodied years later in Elena.

The narrative of Von Cosel's ghost-written autobiography is shaky and jumps about incoherently. He stated that he had visited the United States in his youth and that he had been detained at Ellis Island until one of his sisters, then living in Elizabeth, New Jersey, came up with a $20,000 bond. After that, he continued to live in New York City for about a year, but returned to Germany, his birthplace, to see his mother.

In another section of his autobiography he stated that he served as an assistant in plastic surgery in German hospitals, a claim somewhat substantiated by his monthly checks issued by Reich Credit until 1939, when the Nazis took over the German government at the beginning of World War II. Yet the eccentric narrator vowed that he was interned in Australia during World War I. It is possible that his plastic surgery work was done after the close of World War I when German military patients were still undergoing treatment, but this was not clarified. There was also a rumor that he was paid by the German government for an invention.

He asserted that he had gone to Australia 13 years before World War I, about 1901. He recalled having been in Genoa, Italy, a decade before the advent of World War I, approximately 1904. He claimed it was then that Elena appeared to him in a vision in compos santos among the statuary.

Despite the gaps in his story, it can only be supposed that if Tanzler was interned in Australia, he did return to Germany at the close of World War I, in 1918 or 1919, and worked and lived there until his move to the United States. It has been confirmed that he sailed from Holland in the winter of 1926, presumably to visit a sister who lived in Zephyrhills, near Tampa, Florida. Anyway, he arrived in Cuba on February 6, 1926.

The ferry from Havana brought Tanzler-von Cosel to Key West on March 1, 1926. He must have gone over to the west coast of Florida at some time during that year, for he reputedly bought an orange grove near Tampa in 1927. Nevertheless, it was during this time that Tanzler secured a job at the Marine Hospital in Key West as an X-ray technician. He also announced that he was a pathologist.

That Von Cosel's sexual preference ran to the extreme was testified to by Dr. Ralph Greene, medical director for Eastern Airlines. Dr. Greene made a study of the Von Cosel case and asserted that Von Cosel had an impaired and morbid mentality, a technical trend known as necrophilia, or "marked insane love for the dead." Somewhere in his childhood there was a complex source for his mentally warped condition, which expanded through passing decades on into his maturity.

Part of Tanzler's abnormal condition was revealed in information from his former wife, Doris Tanzler, who was a nurse living in Michigan at the time he was taken into custody in Key West. She sent a letter to a Monroe County Deputy at the time of the Tanzler-von Cosel hearing, which testified: "He is my husband and we have been separated for eleven years. His mind is troubled on account of many ways." She was German and expressed herself thus.

In a more specific revelation of Tanzler's behavior, it was reported that he preferred his wife to ice her body, powder it dead white, and put purple eyeshadow and shade on the flesh of her face, then lie absolutely still during intercourse. In truth, he preferred at least a mock dead partner to a live one. This was undoubtedly the strong motivation for possession of the dead Elena.

Plans to acquire the body of his dying inamorata were made in advance by the necrophiliac. Although he concealed his actual motives, he created several plaster facial masks and at least one face-and-bust cast of Elena while she was still living. He also salvaged the fuselage of a wrecked airplane and established it on the grounds of the Naval Station adjacent to the Marine Hospital.

Elena died on October 16, 1931, about 5 P.M. Dr. Harry Galey examined the deceased and signed the required death certificate. The body was then turned over to the Pritchard Funeral Home in preparation for burial. Presumably the body was embalmed according to regulations, and a wake was held.

It is at this point that the mystery began to evolve. The late Harold Cruz, who was attached to the funeral parlor, and who later worked for the Lopez Funeral Home, claims that Elena's body was never buried at all, but that von Cosel, in a secret maneuver, contrived to substitute a plaster replica for the body. Thus, it was the replica that was buried in the city cemetery plot. Furthermore, Cruz said that von Cosel managed to spirit his love away and that he hid the body in the old plane fuselage on the Navy property. There are a number of other Key Westers who support the contention that this monumental hoax was continued from 1931 through the autumn of 1940.

Among the people who are convinced that von Cosel had engaged in the switch of an effigy for the cadaver was Bienvenido Perez, a police officer who had been a close friend of Elena.

Perez told how he discovered the real body of the dead girl only five months after her passing away. He had been patrolling the area near the Marine Hospital and was curious about the plane in the yard. But every time he went near it von Cosel threatened him.

Despite von Cosel's dire warning that the plane was electrically charged, Perez rolled a barrel over to the plane after von Cosel had left. Standing on the barrel, he peered into the plane and saw something like a covered body lying on a bunk.

"So I went inside the plane via a ladder. I got a scare when I first pulled back the canvas cover. There was Elena! It was easy to recognize her. von Cosel had put in glass eyes, and they stared at me wide open. Also, there was her long, black hair. There was no odor. The body was carefully wrapped in strips of gauze and a kind of cotton cloth, wound around like a mummy, but with the face showing.

"I touched the arms and legs, and they were soft under the wrapping, but the shoulders and hands were dry like a mummy's."

Patrolman Perez swore that he notified Florinda Mesa, Elena's sister, and told her what he had found. She replied that he was mistaken, that what he had seen was only a reproduction in plaster. Perez was unable to convince the sister or any other member of the family, so the matter was dropped.

About this time a new commanding officer at the Naval Station refused to allow von Cosel to keep the plane on Navy property. Since von Cosel had to keep the body concealed, he had the plane, with clumsy wing attachments, towed through the streets to a place on Rest Beach known as Butcher's Pen.

According to Perez, he again warned the sister that Elena's corpse was still in the plane. Again he was ignored. He said, "The family could not think of the old man as a sexual maniac. They thought of him only as a benefactor. One of the relatives even drove the truck which towed the plane to Butcher's Pen, a slaughter house site near Rest Beach."

The late Raul Vasquez, shell collector and restaurant proprietor of Raul's, which was a gathering place for townspeople and for debutante parties, had retired and was almost blind when I interviewed him in August 1952. He said, "I used to have long talks with von Cosel, a very smart man. I know he was crazy, but he was kind, too.

"I saw her body over at his house when he moved to Flagler, but I said nothing, because he worshiped her as a goddess. He used to play the organ he had built in the bedroom. When I was there he told me to look through the gauze curtain he had over the bed, and said, 'Now when I play her favorite piece, you will see her smile.'"

On some nights von Cosel walked all the way from his haphazard abode to Raul's place on South Roosevelt Boulevard to coax Raul to come and see the improvement his efforts had achieved. "She is gaining weight now," von Cosel claimed. "My experiments will work."

Vasquez never told anyone about what he knew until after von Cosel himself was gone. "I felt sorry for this aged man who was brilliant but unbalanced."

For two years after Elena's death, von Cosel, with his own hands, worked on building an elaborate above-ground vault in the city cemetery to house the "body" of his beloved. The low rounded top was capped by an urn and on one corner of the outside wall was the inscription "Elena Hoyos." (Her married name, Mesa, was omitted.) Beneath that her dates of birth and death were followed, ironically, by the traditional "R.I.P."

The burial chamber resembled a low fallout shelter. In its dim interior there was a casket enclosed in a glass-topped case, flanked by a low table and chairs. Von Cosel often sat there "communicating" with Elena. He even left tender love notes to further the illusion that the corpse was in the cemetery shrine. It was rumored, falsely, that he had a telephone in the tomb and conversed with Elena from his house in stormy weather.

On September 29, 1940, Elena's sister, Mrs. Maria Medina, went to Justice of the Peace Enrique Esquinaldo. Very much upset, she told Esquinaldo that she placed flowers on the graves of her family every Sunday, but that suddenly, when she came to Elena's tomb, she had a feeling that her sister was not inside the vault.

Bolstered by her "woman's intuition," she went out to the home of von Cosel and bravely confronted him, asking directly, "What have you done with my sister?"

According to Judge Esquinaldo, the "scientist" admitted he was keeping Elena with him, but he said that he was doing so in order to conduct experiments for restoring her to life. He even showed Mrs. Medina the figure of Elena, lying in state under the bed veiling.

At first Mrs. Medina wanted to hide the truth, so a week's reprieve was given to von Cosel on the condition that he return the body to the cemetery immediately. When he did not comply with the Judge's order, Enrique Esquinaldo urged Mrs. Medina to take legal action. When she finally consented, scandal or no, Esquinaldo obtained a search warrant and an ambulance. On October 6, 1940, he returned to the grisly scene, accompanied by local doctors and members of the sheriffs office.

Von Cosel was taken into custody and placed in the Monroe County jail under a $1,000 bond. He was confined to a single cell. He declaimed that the spirit of Elena visited him there, talked with him, and begged him to bring her back home with him when he could.

Before the corpse, attired in semi-bridal array, was taken to the Lopez Funeral Home, it was examined by most local physicians and a number of other eye-witnesses. Among the stunned viewers was the artist, Belle Anti, then the wife of Dr. Julio dePoo. She later confirmed evidence seen at the site: Von Cosel had not just been "treating" or "worshipping" the partially restored cadaver. He had been cohabiting with it. Physicians who examined the "image" also verified the physical proof–sheets stiff with dried semen–of abnormal behavior by the acknowledged lover of the dead.

The first news coverage, however, played down the truth of von Cosel's monstrous aberration. As a result, many people believed that he was simply a tragic figure, a romantic man who continued a mystic attachment and adoration even after death had come to his sweetheart.

When the "preserved" body was carried from the von Cosel dwelling into the funeral home, it was put on exhibit. Townspeople, by the hundreds, viewed the body. In addition, throngs of the morbidly curious came from all over the United States and from several foreign countries. The total number of viewers was estimated at 6,850!

Among the members of the press who came was the late Jeanne Bellamy of Miami, who wrote of Elena's appearance: "She wore a blue rayon robe, and there was a square of gauze over the chalky face with its glass eyes. There was a matted wig on the skull. The hip bones protruded sharply and the legs, encased in stockings, were like sticks."

Dr. William Warren, a prominent Key West physician, said: "A repaired skeleton was the foundation with some bones wired together. The substitute material had been modeled on the bones, some decayed and others decaying. The frame was wrapped in gauze and other absorbent material."

A hearing was scheduled for October 8, two days after von Cosel's arrest. At the hearing von Cosel was astonished by the furor caused by his possession of a cadaver, and he solemnly announced: "I took her home with me because she was my wife. She had accepted my proposal of marriage. I have so informed the German government."

Von Cosel also protested the removal of Elena's remains from his keeping. Lewis A. Harris, the defense attorney, asked: "Did you have the idea that her spirit would unite with her body and commune with you?"

Von Cosel replied, "And so it did, many times! She gave me advice, even technical advice about the pipe organ. I kept it by her bed so that she could hear the music. It was beneficial and soothing for her, and her ears could hear."

Harris asked, "How would it affect you if the body were taken away from you?"

The reply was emotional. "I would feel lost! I promised her I would keep and protect her the rest of my life, even with my own life, against destruction."

A sanity examination was conducted on October 10. Curiously, despite the testimony heard previously, two doctors and a Mrs. Gilmore Park judged von Cosel to be sane.

On October 11, 1940, Enrique Esquinaldo ordered that von Cosel be tried before a jury of six men for "removal of a corpse from the cemetery and keeping the reconstructed body for more than seven years (it was actually nearly nine) and "wantonly and maliciously disturbing a certain tomb and grave." Said Esquinaldo, "Possession of a body was continued in violation of the law."

On October 12, having spent four days in custody, he was released when the $1000 bond was posted by Joseph Zorsky, a former daredevil circus performer who owned tourist cottages at Cactus Terrace, and Benjamin Fernandez, a restaurant owner.

The "grave robber" hid out at the Cactus Terrace retreat until October 19, when he went back to his home, where he resumed repair on a damaged pipe organ.

Although the vandalism case against von Cosel was to resume on November 11, it was finally dismissed from criminal court. In the meantime, a number of psychiatrists attending a convention in Jacksonville visited Key West to examine von Cosel. He was declared a true necrophiliac, compelled by a rare form of insanity.

In subsequent revelations, von Cosel testified to his preservation techniques: "I rebuilt lost parts and bandaged broken parts. Some of the destroyed parts had to come out, but I replaced these with beeswax and Plaster of Paris, and I put on sufficient absorbent material so that I could soak her in the solutions to feed her and develop tissues. I was very careful. I used a preservative and powerful germicide called Clinosol to bathe Elena. It cost fifteen dollars an ounce, and had to be ordered from Hamburg, Germany."

All of this information was divulged in "lectures" which von Cosel later gave to thousands of paying sightseers who toured his laboratory off Flagler Avenue.He charged twenty-five cents a head and sold picture postcards of the scene. This continued for six months. There was even a film made of the conducted tour. In his lecture series, von Cosel expounded his theory that "Life is dormant and simply inactive in a dead person. Life can be awakened by a series of treatments by chemical solutions which penetrate perforations in the body and feed the cells. There are many perforations. I had to submerge the whole body in the solution I prepared."

The tumble-down dwelling where he conducted the tours consisted of two sections or cubicles. The front one held X-ray machine parts and some of the "treatment" apparatus, odds and ends of laboratory equipment, plus a container, which he said was a vat for immersing the body, used in the experiments for restoration of ruined tissues.

In the second area of the home was a very narrow walking space around the bed in which Von Cosel had trysted with his deceased "bride." A semi-concealing canopy of gauze (some said that it was flimsy cheesecloth instead of mosquito netting) was suspended over the bedstead. Next to that was the keyboard of a pipe organ which he had constructed from a damaged one obtained from a church. Up on a corner shelf, he had placed a large portrait photo of Elena in a wedding veil. On the wall was a death mask, cowled in white with a blue headband.

The reporter who observed these details also noted that the front door of the shabby place had a sign reading "Laboratory." The yard was overgrown with tall grass and weeds, half hiding a sundial. The plane fuselage in which von Cosel had concealed the body was also in the yard. The nose of the place was painted with the title "CTS Elena von Cosel." The CTS before the name "Elena" stood for Countess.

As for what was left of the unfortunate Elena, the bones were sawed into small pieces and, along with the plaster, beeswax, wrapped gauze and foam rubber portions, were deposited in a small casket. This was reburied one night at 3 A.M., under cover of darkness. Rumors have it that the unmarked grave is beneath one of the roads in the city cemetery, but only Harold Cruz, the last surviving member of the reburial squad, knew for certain, and he died in September, 1980.

These cautious measures were taken because Elena's relatives feared that von Cosel might somehow again get hold of the remains and commit further "sacrileges."

Some friends continued to be loyal to the "mad genius," but many islanders feared his presence in the community. Hence, he was evicted from the property on Flagler Avenue and, in the spring of 1941, "exiled" from Key West.

Four hours after von Cosel's departure for Zephyrhills, Florida–his choice of place to spend his exile–the tomb dedicated to the memory of Elena was rocked by an explosion. The vault was damaged but not completely destroyed. It was not until a few years ago that the crypt was demolished, reportedly to prevent curiosity seekers from further effacing the structure. Visitors to the site, through the years, had been in the habit of chipping off chunks of the mausoleum and trampling nearby graves.

On August 13, 1952, Karl Tanzler-von Cosel's decomposed body was discovered in a small house about two miles from Zephyrhills. Coroner L.L. Jones of Zephyrhills testified that death apparently was due to natural causes of advanced age. A search of the house led to the discovery of death masks and a life-sized image of the lost Elena. Thus, eleven years after he was "exiled" from Key West, Karl Tanzler, minus his titles of doctor and of nobility, was buried in the Zephyrhills area. Rather than being laid to rest beside his beloved Elena, he was entombed next to his own daughter. The fact that he had children was disclosed only after he had left Key West.

TWEETHEART

St. Valentine's Day is the most widely observed day in the month of February. Of course, there is Ground Hog Day, February 2, but it doesn't have romantic appeal. And there are birthdays for Presidents Lincoln and Washington to be marked. But St. Valentine's Day remains the most popular with its hearts entwined theme–and not just for people!

February 14 is a day designated as one for the birds–at least for canaries in South Florida. Breeders of the songbirds usually arrange for mating season to begin then, and there is a mass marriage of birds of a feather who are caged together. I suppose this schedule is coordinated with the most advantageous time to coincide with bird show and market dates, for the mating period actually can wing in any time when spring is in the air.

I first learned about the official "Tweetheart Day" some years ago when I was on the *Key West Citizen* staff. I received a phone call asking me if I was interested in Red Factors. For a few minutes I wondered if somebody was stirring up the ghosts of a Communist witch hunt.

As the conversation continued, I learned that a Red Factor had nothing to do with the Russians. It was a color characteristic in the genes of a new type of canary. The caller, Suzie Michalk, who lived on Fogarty Avenue, had just won six trophies and a number of show prize ribbons for exhibiting her champions at an international Red Factor Breeders Association premiere show, the first in all the world. Mrs. Michalk invited me to come see the winning birds and have an interview.

I had never had much experience with canaries, although my grandmother had two in gilded cages. One was a ball of fluffy butter-yellow, a chopper, as the somewhat ordinary breed is known, and an olive-yellow bird with black marking, a Hartz Mountain roller introduced from Germany. He was a marvel, initiating his songs with a bass tone, then rolling into flute notes, something called "Glucke tours," and a bubbling water effect, with variations.

I appreciated Billie's nearly operatic roller achievements, but found Dickie's loud, short bursts and trilling more interesting, chiefly because he had been captured by my grandmother. She had invented a sort of Rube Goldberg contraption to catch him. She spied the little canary hopping round in the yard, obviously a lost pet unused to uncaged freedom and looking for a handout.

She scattered a trail of seeds from the back walk to a feeding area inside our latticed back porch. Over this, she suspended the top of a round cage on a thin cord. When the canary followed the seed trail to the center of the cage bottom, she snipped the cord and the upper cage dropped, encasing the hungry bird.

She had taken a teasing from my grandfather, who had taunted her about getting close to the bird. "As you know, the only way to catch it, according to an old saying, is to put salt on the bird's tail." She exhibited her prize and collected a bet of $10. Dickie lived to a venerable thirteen years, although eight is the average life span for a canary.

Back to the prospective feature on Red Factors. Al Palmer, from Montreal, was our photographer at the time, and all the way to the Michalk house, he sang French love ditties and whistled tunefully. He claimed it was to get into the mood for bird mating photos.

A black and white mongrel dog greeted us with friendly overtures when we got out of the car and approached the Michalk residence. But the instant we stepped inside the house-aviary, a furious chorus of bird noises began. The clamor never let up the entire hour or so that we were there. There were chirps, trills warbles, cheeps, clucks, whistles and bird chatter interchanged, and this came from more than three hundred throbbing throats! Besides the canaries, dozens of parakeets, some capable of talking, unleashed their vocal abilities. The resulting cacophony was incredible.

The owner of this filibustering bird congress, Mrs. Michalk, said that the birds would begin sounding off if even a beetle crawled near the caged inmates.

Photographer Palmer asked, "Doesn't all that racket bother you at night?"

"No," said Mrs. Michalk with a saucy tilt to her head, just like a perky canary, "but if you came around you might bother the birds. They are regular little watchdogs, and set up a disturbance whenever anyone or anything strange intrudes into the bird colony."

The bird woman claimed that her canaries were individuals with distinctive personalities. "There are shy birds and bold ones: some are aloof and others are friendly. I've been in the bird business for eighteen years, and I can study a person a short while and know what kind of bird is for them. Some want a bright colored bird with a soft song. Some want a standard bird with a loud song. My advice is listen to the bird and its song before buying. I don't sell birds to just anybody."

In order to make a canary more tuneful, a special diet must be fed. Suzie Michalk said that, in addition to a variety of seeds, the trillers ate lawn grass, dandelion leaves, carrots, yeast, endive, watercress, broccoli, escarole, and small amounts of lettuce, plus cooked egg yolk, and apple and orange tidbits. Cuttlebone is also placed in the cages.

A favorite bird seed is from Indian hemp, which is also known as Bhang or marijuana! Give a bird enough hemp and it will hang itself–even upside down–from its perch in acrobatic postures. Cannabis sativa, besides yielding a coarse fiber used in cordage, is also the basis of the narcotic hashish.

The warblers were originally bred in the Canary Islands and were a light to moderate yellow. Since then, crossbreeding with finches, siskins, bullfinches, linnets, and relative species, the colors vary in shades of buff, fawn, copper, cinnamon, brown, orange, pure white, chartreuse, olive green, light green, avocado, slate blue, and even pastel pink.

The champion Red Factors raised in Key West included fine feathered friends in shrimp pink, apricot, and tomato red. Markings were in brown and black on wings and tail, and very stylish birds had frosted feathers, touches of white on the surface, like

milady's frosted hair coloring!

The carolers were confined to tiers of rectangular cages. In one compartment, there were 115 female canaries, all contentedly chirping and tweeting, doubtless gossiping bird-style, discussing potential husbands and clutches. A clutch is not a grip or part of a motor vehicle in birddom. It's the number of eggs laid by a canary hen. The average clutch is four eggs.

To keep things under control, the breeder removes the first egg of the clutch and swaddles it in cotton wool, placing this in a warming container. The first egg is not replaced in the nest until the other eggs have been laid. This is to keep the first hatched bird from getting the edge on the later arrivals.

The Key West birds included "mules," and readers may get a kick out of the fact that "mules" in the bird world are like mules in the animal realm–they are hybrids and can't reproduce their kind.

Ladies and gentlemen of plumage are kept in separate quarters until the mating session is due. The hen is into women's lib. She makes the overtures, Leap Year or not, calling to the male, crouching and fluttering her wings. The male is separated by a wire slide in the double breeder cage. If he is in prime, fit condition, he begins to sing "lustily," as one reference said with unconscious punning. Then the barrier wire is removed and the mating proceeds.

We witnessed only one St. Valentine's Day courtship. Duchess, a canary of Cuban lineage–and very warm-blooded, said Mrs. Michalk–was wooing her cage mate with coy posturing and very dainty, feather-touch flirting techniques, which more than did justice to the Southern Belle tradition.

Pinkie, the selected male, did not seem in the pink of condition for romance, and did not even twitch a pinion.

Perhaps Pinkie was reserved in his behavior, for even a bird bridegroom could be hesitant with strangers observing the overture to nuptials. Duchess, however, was a shameless hussy in her performance.

There were three rare and curious-looking canaries in the collection, identified as Closters. The birds sported a feathery fringe on top of their their heads. Their feathers encircled the crown and hung down in bangs to just over their eyes. The effect was laughable, like a Dutch Bob fright wig worn by one of the comedians in the Three Stooges movies.

As Palmer and I left the premises, a trained parakeet named Pretty Boy whistled loudly and called, "Hello, baby! Give me a kiss!"

I hopped out to the car all a-twitter.

CARNIVAL CAPER

Charity isn't the only thing that begins at home. So does trouble!

Key West, in the early winter and spring of 1953, was a prime example. The annual Navy Relief Carnival opened to the public officially on February 18, with the usual zest involving the entire community, military and civilian. The aim was to raise a larger quota than ever before, with the money from the shows and concessions to go to the Navy Relief Fund.

The monies obtained for this notable cause were distributed to various Navy Benefits: loans of money to needy Navy families was the first consideration. To the saying, "The Navy Takes Care Of Its Own," might be added, "With a Little Help From Friends." In this case, the friends were local citizens of Key West, and they were more than willing to help in financial contributions to Navy Relief, which dealt with service personnel numbering in the thousands.

Camaraderie between civilians and military groups reached a zenith during Carnival days. Townspeople flocked to the various benefits, parties and shows promoted by the Navy, the predominant military component back then. The Coast Guard and the U.S. Marine Corps were, of course, part of the campaign recipients, but there was no strong Army unit here.

The growing Naval Air Station was the most expanding unit of the military, and so the staff of the Naval Air Station at Boca Chica and the Seaplane Base were designated as the leading force in the drive for funds. Capt. A.E. Buckley was commanding officer of NAS, serving under Rear Admiral Irving T. Duke, the commanding officer of the entire Naval Base.

That was a memorable period in military circles. A wave of patriotism crested when native Key Wester Capt. Manuel "Pete" Fernandez, flying ace of the Korean conflict, came home to a hero's welcome, here as well as in Miami, and the Armed Forces parade and celebration was the largest in the history of the island.

In the same time niche, Ernest Hemingway reappeared in Key West in the middle of June, his first visit to Key West since 1947. All in all, it seemed an auspicious year.

Mayor C.B. Harvey worked diligently for harmony between the civilian populace and the military residents. There was a fine rapport between city, county and Navy officials. In fact, that's why a number of local politicians accepted the Navy's invitation to attend a special show, a smoker which was separate from the public entertainment to be staged in the big hangar at the Seaplane Base.

The huge hangar was jammed with people who came to try the games of chance, such as attempting to drop a coin onto toy submerged submarines to win a prize; tickets were also sold for the usual gallery-type games, ball throws and booths of ordinary carnival games combining skill and chance.

A steel band was imported from the Caribbean for concerts and dances. Local bands also responded so that music was continuous. A few top entertainers came down from the Miami nightclubs to add professional éclat to the performances: singers, comedians, musical combos, and a popular, famous foursome, The Vagabonds, musicians and singers starring Peter Peterson, a bass player of Swedish and Hawaiian ancestry who featured a risque number. The shows engaged nearly every local entertainer, so the fun and amusement went on from afternoon until late at night. And the shekels rolled in. It was estimated later that the total Navy Relief Carnival take was around $70,000.

But somebody in the upper echelons of Navy officialdom was over-anxious to surpass the relief funds quota. Although the 1953 Navy Carnival was rated a financial success, it became a national scandal due to Washington columnist Drew Pearson's exposé of a charity smoker held February 9, 1953, at the Cuban Club on Duval Street. The revelation of the hanky-panky and a live sex exhibition did not come about until mid-summer. The first installment of Pearson's exposé of the scandalous behavior appeared in his syndicated column on July 1, 1953. Mayor C.B. Harvey immediately received an apology from Pearson. Pearson had named him among the city officials who were allegedly present at the stag spectacular. But the word went around that nearly all the other city and county officials had attended the event.

The proceedings began at 6:30 with a drinking session. Dinner was served at 7:30. After dinner there were pornographic movies, then the "piece de non-resistance," a sex show on-stage with live participants. That Navy personnel of a variety of ranks were present went undisputed. A lot of local residents, not all politicos, also were there. They paid large fees for admittance. After all, the object was to raise funds for Navy Relief benefit.

Up to this date, reports of Naval officer misbehavior, for the most part, had been limited to a few pranks. For example, four junior grade officers had caught a large shark, then put it in the back seat of their car, concealed it under a tarpaulin, and smuggled it past the Marine guard to the officers' swimming pool on the Seaplane Base. After dark, the shark was dumped in the deep end, where it promptly sank to the bottom of the pool. Then the shark-catchers went back to Echoasis, where they spent the hours until closing time with fellow officers before returning to their bachelor officers' quarters. There was no big "Hilton-type" BOQ then. Only several barracks-like buildings.

One young officer got up early on the morning-after, still a little groggy, and decided a Sunday morning dip in the pool would be refreshing. So he pulled on swimming trunks, clambered over the fence and dived in. In the pool depths he opened his eyes and spotted a huge fish, but attributed the vision to his hangover.

He surfaced, then dived again, this time approaching the shadowy bulk in the water, and reached to touch it. Sure enough, the raspy hide was that of a seven-foot hammerhead. He hastily swam up and practically jumped out of the pool to report the shark.

At first his alarm was laughed at. He was told to sober up. But investigation proved him right. The shark was real, though dead. The NAS captain closed the pool until the culprits confessed. They were ordered to remove the offending shark, they had swimming privileges taken from them, and they were subjected to minor disciplinary measures.

Comment was, "Boys will be boys."

But the new offense of the carnival "Star Smoker" elicited the observation, "Men will be men, but not so as to disgrace the Navy."

Columnist Pearson related the happenings in full, although some of the juicier aspects were not described in detail. The grapevine in Key West worked overtime, and the whole town knew the sequence, although at first the investigation was difficult, since a lot of Key Westers clammed up, as did service people, except amidst their own circles, with only hints about the true circumstances.

However, higher-ups in Washington set up a court martial procedure, with trial to be held in Charleston, South Carolina. Charges were brought against Lt. Cmdr. Gerry McDaniel, who was accused of "disobedience of a lawful ordinance and conduct unbecoming of an officer and a gentleman." He was apparently the instigator of the smoker.

Capt. A.E. Buckley, commanding officer of the Naval Air Station, suffered a heart attack and was hospitalized. Rear Admiral Irving T. Duke, in command of the entire Naval Base, was shortly afterward transferred to another post, replaced by Rear Adm. George C.

Turner.

The actual trial site was moved from Charleston to Pensacola, Florida. McDaniel, who had been arrested in March, was held for forty days, incommunicado. Seven enlisted men were sent to the brig here. The men claimed that they only acted under orders and that the charges brought against them were cover-ups for higher officials. The public was inclined to agree.

One of the enlisted men involved was Chief Lee Lawlor, now deceased, who became a Marine Patrol Officer after leaving the Navy. He told me personally that he was ordered by his superior officers to go out to Stock Island and pick up two prostitutes and deliver them to the Cuban Club on the night of February 9.

His terse comment was, "I did as I was told; arrangements had already been made by an officer to enlist the girls for the show."

At the court-martial, "Sheilah the Peelah" was called on to testify as to her part in the sex act, courtesy of Mom's Tea Room. She showed up draped in an expensive mink coat and nonchalantly answered questions on the stand, interspersing testimony with pungent remarks. When one of the prosecutors demeaned her "profession" she haughtily declaimed, "My work brings me a very good living." She smoothed the luxuriant fur of her coat and asked the questioning attorney saucily, "Could *you* afford an expensive mink like this?" The courtroom erupted in laughter.

What actually transpired on stage at the Cuban Club has been related with variations on an old theme. But the main tune was that besides the porno films, a line of striptease "artists" from the Havana-Madrid Club danced through several numbers to enthusiastic cries of "Take it off!" They all complied in turn. But the manager of the Front Street strip joint, where Old Town Square is now located, says he and his "girls" left early in order to appear at the Havana-Madrid on time for the regular strip show.

After another interlude when drinks were dispensed, mattresses were dragged from the wings to stage center. The main performer, "Sheilah the Peelah," appeared, and after a disrobing routine, challenged the audience. "Anybody want to wrestle?" she called. Although she pronounced it "wrassle," the meaning was clear. The cost was reportedly $50 a throw and no holds barred.

A lusty sailor, who could justly be branded as having "hornpipe fever," was happy to respond, but he claimed he didn't have the wherewithal–the money, that is. So his buddies, who had urged him on, took up a collection, and the necessary fifty bucks was raised for the volunteer participant to get into the act.

He was a dogged individual and insisted that his participation in the onstage performance would be in keeping with his moonlighting job. When he wasn't on Navy duty, he was assistant to a local veterinarian, and his specialty was care of canines.

His exhibition was dedicated to his knowledge of dog behavior, while he howled "Bitch!" over and over again.

One voyeur shrugged and said, "Just animal spirits."

The smoker turned out to be a hot time in the old town that night, such a one as was rarely, if ever or since, provided.

Navy Chief Futterer was in charge of the invitations to the Cuban Club fun and games for February 9, and it was announced at the time of the court-martial that the list of invitations would be made public. It was expected that names of people in unofficial capacity would be revealed, too. However, there were conflicts and denials by so many of the local men that the list was not certified.

An account of the trial appeared August 14. It was held before Capt. Charon Murphy, Naval Station Chief of Staff. Attorney J.Y. Porter IV, native Conch and ex-Naval officer, was present with two stenographers and one reporter, Jim Cobb of the *Citizen*.

Boatswain's Mate Raymond Robinson was found guilty of two charges in connection with the "Star Smoker." One charge was "entering the Stock Island bawdy house," which was off limits for the Navy. He was restrained in the Naval Base for thirty days and paid a hundred-dollar fine. Pandering charges were later dropped. Light fines and brief jail terms were handed out to other enlisted Navy men. Lt. Cmdr. McDaniel "beat the rap" with a severe reprimand and forfeiture of service pay.

BITTER TEA
(SUICIDE AT MOM'S)

Mom's Tea Room had a cozy sound to its name, but it wasn't everyone's cup of tea. It was a well-known establishment for prostitution, located on Stock Island in a grove of palm trees.

Mom's flourished for years and was a favorite hangout for the military, even though it had been declared off-limits by the powers that be. The structure looked quite sedate on the outside, like a turn-of-the-century bungalow-farmhouse with an encircling porch and a backyard. There were no chickens on the grounds; however, the birds inside were of a more exotic kind.

True or not, there was a funny legend connected with the bawdy house, which was located in the vicinity of the residence of Key West's city manager, Dave King. The story went that a visiting admiral and his lady, from Washington, D.C., went to Stock Island to pay a courtesy call on Dave King. Their official car was driven by a Navy man new to the area, at least to Stock Island and environs.

The Navy driver went to Mom's Tea Room instead of the city manager's abode! He was sent to the door of the dwelling with an engraved card bearing the name of the visiting VIP, with instructions to give it to the maid to place in the calling card tray. There were reports that the admiral's card later was shown as evidence that Mom's Tea Room was an elite, accepted place of assignation.

I was on the staff of the *Key West Citizen,* and I reported for work early the morning of January 6, 1952. Publisher Norman Artman notified me that I had an immediate assignment on Stock Island. Jokingly I said, "No doubt I'm to go after a story about Mom's Tea Room." Much to my surprise, my boss replied, "That's right! How did you guess?"

Then he *told* me, as they once kidded about those World War II educational movies. I learned fast!

There was a report of a murder at Mom's, I was to go to Stock Island and get the story. The problem was in obtaining a car. This was in the days when both the *Citizen* staff and resources for transportation were limited. It was suggested that I contact the *Miami Herald* representative, Adon Taft (now the *Herald's* religion writer), and also take along Lew McClain, a free-lance photographer.

I hurried to the Southernmost Hotel on Duval Street to rouse Taft.

He came into the lobby looking disgruntled, since it was only around 7:30 A.M. and too early for his usual assignment time. But he perked up when I told him of the murder rumor.

In the hotel lobby was a middle-aged man, somewhat heavy-set, who wore horn-rimmed glasses which did not conceal his alert eyes. He, too, perked up, all attention, when he heard our conversation. He got up from his chair and introduced himself.

"Excuse me for butting in," he said, "but I am Croswell Bowan of *The New Yorker* magazine. I write the crime section (the magazine had one at that time), and I couldn't help overhearing about your mission. I'm up early to go aboard a shrimp trawler, but I think a murder in a house of ill fame would be much more exciting and right up my alley. Could I possibly trail along with you?"

We agreed to take Bowan with us. There was only one drawback. The writer was lame, and he slowed us up as we rushed about. However, his helpful advice somewhat offset the handicap.

We picked up McClain and his camera first, then drove out to Mom's Tea Room, located off McDonald Avenue in a quiet section of the island. The establishment was shuttered and peaceful as we drove past it two or three times, and then investigated the back section of the property, which was also devoid of any sound or movement.

The astute *New Yorker* writer advised that we seek the nearest all-night bar, Wylk's, and do a little advance query. "After all," he pointed out, "places like Mom's don't open at such early hours. They probably just closed before dawn, and everyone is asleep."

The scouting trip continued. Sure enough, the Wylk's bartender, "Mickey Mouse" Rodriguez, had information to impart. He said that the whole neighborhood knew that a girl named Rita, who was employed at the Tea Room, had been taken to the hospital the night before at about half past nine, but that she hadn't been killed by anyone.

Said Mickey Mouse, "She took an overdose of sleeping pills, they say."

We made another trip to Mom's and parked around in the rear of the premises. Bowan said that a woman might gain admittance easier than a man, so I was delegated to venture the approach while the men stayed in the car.

I knocked at the back entrance after opening the screen door on the frame porch. At the third attempt an answer came. A stocky, gray-haired man opened the door a few inches and peered at me. He spotted the three male occupants of the car, sized me up, and evidently assumed that I had come out to the house for a party. At least that's what Bowan said afterward.

Anyway, he opened the wooden door further, and I went part way into a room that was the kitchen.

"You're a little early for action," he said.

"I'd like to speak to the, ah… madame… that is, the manager," I explained.

"She's asleep. You can't talk to her," the man said. "I'm in charge right now,"

I asked his name, and he grinned.

"My name is Hi Mister. Everybody calls me that. Just Hi Mister."

He flashed a huge yellow diamond on his little finger as he waved his hand airily and asked, "Just what did you have in mind? Maybe arrangements could be made for your party later on.

At that point, Taft, Bowan and McClain piled out of the automobile, and Hi Mister scrutinized them as they crossed the yard and came toward the porch. However, they never got any further. Hi Mister saw McClain's camera and suddenly realized we were a press party. He shoved me backward, nearly all the way outside. I stuck my foot in the door, though, and he couldn't quite close it.

My escorts stood outside, and Taft said, "We just want to talk to you about what happened here last night. We heard there was a killing, and then we heard the death was a suicide of one of the… ah… employees."

Bowan began the buttering up. "You look like an intelligent fellow. You can help us. Why don't you come out on the porch and give us some information?"

Hi Mister responded and walked out, closing the door firmly behind him. "Okay," he said, "but I really don't know much about the girl. Her name was Rita Rogers, but I guess that was not her real moniker because she was Portuguese. All I know for sure is that she's dead. They didn't take her to the hospital in an ambulance. When she was found about 9:30 P.M., somebody, never mind who, rushed her off to the hospital in a car. I don't know if she was dead then or not."

Hi Mister turned out to be talkative once he got started. "Rita was a nervous type. Quiet and sort of timid. You must remember she wasn't living a normal life." At this statement Croswell Bowan snorted and commented, "That's an understatement, you can bet."

"Well, Rita just got back from Miami about two days ago, and she kept moaning around that she wanted to die. She didn't really like men. She was a thesbian."

"Don't you mean a Lesbian?" I asked.

The diamond glittered in the morning sun as Hi Mister gestured and shrugged. "Whatever she was, she had a fight with her girl friend here, and she was fed up with life. You see, she had to work here, too, if she wanted to be with her girl friend. Since she didn't go for men at all, it got to be too much for her, I guess."

He gave some final valuable information, revealing the name of the doctor the girl had called in the afternoon on Sunday. He said that Rita was now at a local funeral parlor, where we could also find the ambulance driver who had brought her from the hospital.

At the funeral home, the ambulance driver said his knowledge was limited, and that the girl was already dead when admitted to the emergency room, where a stomach pump had been used to no avail.

Calling from the funeral parlor to the hospital was frustrating. The nurse said, "The girl you speak of was not a patient here. She was dead when brought in. Check with the funeral home." Which was where my call was being made!

However, the undertaker was more cooperative. "The body was brought here around 11:30 last night. When I talked to the coroner, he said to just keep the corpse and not do anything until the death certificate had been signed and that he would let me know when it was. So about midnight the call came through, and the coroner told me to go ahead and embalm. I didn't even know the victim's name or what funeral arrangements were to be made. Somebody said the woman's folks were in Portland, Maine. I have the body ready for shipment."

He asked if we would like to view the body, and we were escorted into a room where there was a wheeled table bearing a sheet-covered form. The attendant stripped down the sheet. The unclad woman lay in repose with arms folded across her chest. Her features were aquiline and rather severe looking. The mouth was firm even in the finality of death. The figure was trim and well modeled, about five feet, four inches in length. The dark brown hair was cut in a mannish bob.

As we grouped around the table, somebody murmured, "Pretty good-looking babe, wasn't she?"

We drove over to Whitehead Street from the funeral home to discuss the case with the coroner. He was on the telephone when the press unit paraded in, and from the tail end of the one-sided conversation we learned that he was in touch with the funeral home and had been alerted to our arrival.

96

The coroner began on a defensive note. "I don't know much about the affair. You'll have to talk to her physician. He was taking care of this woman, and he signed the death certificate. If this is deemed a suspicious death, then we'll turn the case over to the sheriffs office. Otherwise, it's just routine."

I was bold enough to question this. "Don't you consider a suicide a suspicious death–not routine?"

The coroner, Roy Hamlin, hedged. "Can't say whether this death is a suicide or not. Whatever she died of is on the death certificate. I haven't seen it. Now look, I am a busy man. Better talk to her physician, Dr. Aubrey Hamilton."

At this stage of the game I was certain we were getting the runaround. But I had to get back to the *Citizen* to write the story. My deadline was noon, and it was nearing 11 A.M. Finally, just before noon, after many tries, I reached Dr. Hamilton at his office.

He had been a physician in the Chinese army, came from Upper New York State, and spoke with a British accent. In clipped, precise tones he said, "Yes, I signed the death certificate. The girl, known as Rita Rogers, died of an overdose of barbiturates. I treated her for a boil several weeks ago when she came in for the regular checkup required in her line of business. She was very despondent, and I advised her to get away from her scene of employment for a while."

He paused, then continued calmly. "I gave her a few sleeping pills to quiet her nerves, but certainly not enough to harm her! I suspect, however, that when she went to Miami, she manipulated the prescription over and over again, somehow, and obtained more barbiturates until she had enough for the fatal dose. I also learned, too late, that she frequently had expressed a death wish. She went on a vacation, the other girls reported, but she did not come back to see me at this office."

The doctor explained that he had warned Rita she would eventually have to undergo surgery for a bilateral ovarian operation. The last time she was in his office was on December 21, 1951, when he had dressed the lanced boil.

On January 6, 1952, the day Rita died, she had called the doctor and aid she was feeling badly after taking some sleeping pills. She did not say she had taken a great many, and the doctor assumed she just felt "dopey."

"After all," he said, "I had prescribed lightly. So I told her to take a taxi to the office and I would give her a benzedrine shot. This was around 2 P.M., and I was entertaining guests for Sunday dinner. It wasn't until ten o'clock that night that I was informed of her death.

It seems she had collapsed right at the telephone, and nobody was up and stirring at the, ah, establishment, at that time of day. Nobody found her until around 9:30 P.M., and it was too late."

Five days passed before Rita's parents came to Key West and claimed their daughter's body. It was learned then that she was twenty-nine years old.

As a result of the newspaper expose, the navy authorities really clamped down and closed Mom's Tea Room. The building later burned to the ground.

TALLULAH

For years, I interviewed the top flight stage, screen and nightclub personalities when I was entertainment editor for the *Miami Daily News*, and in freelancing. I had built up a sort of shield in the effort to be pragmatic about the glamour and charm of personages in show business.

But I reckoned without the personal projection of magnetism which emanated from actress Tallulah Bankhead.

Miss Bankhead came to Key West in the spring of 1960 for rest and relaxation. The "R-and-R" interlude was in preparation for her role in the comedy, *Midgie Purvis*, written by Mary Chase, who had created the prize-winning comedy, *Harvey*.

The popular song, "Stars Fell on Alabama," was based on an actual meteorite shower. After Miss Bankhead glowed on the theatrical horizon, one critic introduced a saying, calling her "The Star That Fell on Alabama." The title was apt! Tallulah was born in Casper, Alabama, the last of January in 1903 (one version has it in 1902), and she had a blazing career. In March and April of 1960, the brilliant star was still illuminating the theatrical world–although she was fifty-seven or fifty-eight and past her prime in comparison with earlier decades.

Tallulah was the house guest of writer James Leo Herlihy, who at that time maintained a home on Johnson Street. Herlihy called me at the *Key West Citizen* and asked if I would like to interview Miss Bankhead. The only stipulation was that the interview was to be informal and that I would not bring a photographer. A picture portrait would be supplied, I was told. The newspaper complied on the request with a minimum of protest.

On a Sunday afternoon in late March, 1960, Herlihy arrived in a little convertible at my abode at 620 Dey Street, and I was driven to the rendezvous with some apprehension on my part.

I need not have had any tremulous feeling. Miss Bankhead was in the front patio with singer Dick Duane and her secretary-companion, Ted Hook, very much at ease, which put me in a parallel mood.

She was wearing casual attire: peacock blue pedal pushers, a shirt–blouse of white with delicate feather design in light blue with deeper touches of blue that matched her eyes. A narrow band of blue ribbon in an exact shade held her tawny mane of hair in an off-the-face frame, a simple coiffure that enhanced the slanted high cheekbones and the sensuous mouth. She wiggled her small, high-arched bare feet in white sandal wedgies as she sat sipping a cocktail.

But it was her voice that entranced. It has been described many times by different writers: "like hot honey and milk" was one scintillating phrasing. Oh, there was no doubt that at one time she was noted for boisterous brawling projection, but that lazy, afternoon in 1960, her tone, though resonant, was subdued. I dreamed up my own description, and in my subsequent article on Tallulah, as she insisted on being called, I referred to her vocalization in purple prose as "velvet thunder."

It was utter magic, and "magic," she confided, was her favorite word. As she talked of other years and other places, and triumphs as well as disappointments, the images of her life were conjured up like... well, "like magic." There were glimpses of the young beauty with a sensitive, almost wistful expression, who conquered England; an ethereal reflection of her portrayal of Camille; of the sultry sophisticate; of the hoidenish comedienne; and, above all, of the proud, haughty vixen in The Little Foxes.

The conversation was interspersed with a succession of "Dahlings," but only a few mild "damns." There was no barrelhouse "cussin'" which she was known to do. The range of topics was so amazing–covering theater critics, politics, books, music, her coming play, in which she had the title role, and her pets, especially her dogs, among them a white Pekinese and a Maltese terrier on her estate in New York. The estate was called "Windows," and she owned it for a long time before giving up the country surroundings for urban living.

While discussing the subject of pets, she learned that I had recently acquired a purebred black and silver German shepherd that was still in the process of learning commands in English. He had been taught by a German trainer, and I had to transpose German orders into English for him for weeks before the change-over was perfected.

I was paying for him on time. The down-payment was a gift from The Players, instigated by Dick Theall, who was then president of the Little Theater movement here and director of *The Sleeping Prince*, then playing at the Barn Theater, the home of Key West Players–a small edifice behind the Women's Club on Duval Street.

Geronimo, as I had named my dog, was a "hearing ear" dog, not by training, but by his innate intelligence. He barked not only as a watchdog when anybody came to the house, but also when the telephone rang. As a guard dog he was superlative. His chief fault was howling when I left him at home.

Tallulah immediately expressed interest. "I'd like to see him. And why don't we go get him? Why leave the poor creature alone?"

She also insisted that I stay "for supper" with her usual Southern hospitality gesture. So off we tooled in Herlihy's little car, back to my apartment to fetch my dog, who weighed in the neighborhood of ninety-five pounds.

Geronimo was usually fierce toward strangers, but Tallulah was fearless. There was instant rapport between them. She was a surprisingly small woman, about five foot-three, and at the time not overweight. The big dog responded to her with adoration. Back at Herlihy's house, Geronimo continued to be enraptured with her attention. She fed him chicken during and after our evening repast, removing bones from the meat with care.

Cuban Consul Oscar Morales and his wife dropped in for a chat. Not a monologist on this occasion at least, Miss Bankhead proved to be an attentive listener to the report of the Cuban situation. She showed great acumen concerning world affairs. The evening ended on an extremely pleasant note, and I was driven home with a feeling of having established a friendship over and beyond the duty of an newspaper interviewer.

During her several weeks' stay here, Tallulah was feted by Tennessee Williams at a party at his Duncan Street home. The two southerners were wary of each other, professionally, but he wrote his play, *The Milk Train Doesn't Stop Here Anymore,* with Tallulah in mind, and it is reported that at one time he had thought of her as Blanche in *Streetcar Named Desire.* At any rate, the party was attended by illustrious locals and visitors, and was a huge success.

One memorable evening, Tallulah, accompanied by Hook, Herlihy, Duane, Danny Stirrup, and dozens of other followers, one of them being David Loovis, the novelist, trooped into a nightclub named "All That Jazz." It was then in the interior of what is now Dedek's Fogarty House. It was known originally as Luigi's and was operated then, in 1960, by New York "immigrants." It was an ultrasmart spot for the town and was frequented by local and visiting writers and celebrities.

Tallulah appeared on stage and gave a throaty rendition, a recitation rather than singing, but a hit performance, presenting old favorites such as "As Time Goes By." She "wowed" the audience, including playwright Williams.

Accompanied by her cohorts, Tallulah attended a performance of *The Sleeping Prince*, in which I had a role as a duchess. She also sent me a telegram with the traditional theatrical greeting, "Break A Leg," for the opening.

Alas, I did not fare well in the review of the play. I was described as "a charwoman masquerading as a duchess." The next day I trudged into *The Citizen* with a mop and pail, for the moment resigned to my ill fate on stage.

A few days after Tallulah left Key West for New York, I received a tremendous surprise. She sent a check for $75 to cover the final amount I owed on the purchase of my dog!

As for her performance in *Midgie Purvis*, which was finally produced and presented February 1, 1961, at the Martin Beck Theater in New York, Tallulah scored a personal triumph once again. For her interpretation of a middle-aged woman who skipped the years between that and old age, portraying an 80-year-old heroine, she was nominated for an Antoinette Perry Award–a "Tony."

She gave me her private telephone number before leaving Key West. So in the summer of 1962, while vacationing in New York City, I called, announced that I was a newspaper columnist Tallulah had known in Key West and asked if I might speak with Miss Bankhead. The booming answer was immediate: "I remember you, Dorothy, This is Tallulah."

Then I pulled the blooper of all time, while my host, David Loovis, collapsed in convulsive laughter in the background. My telephone reply was unwittingly the most ironical on record. I faltered, "Oh, I didn't recognize your voice!"

This in answer to perhaps the most famous vocalization in the whole world!

We didn't manage to have another meeting then, due to conflicting respective engagements, but the friendly exchange via telephone concluded with a promise to have a further encounter in the future. Tallulah had received a copy of the *Key West Citizen* article of April 2, 1960, and was distinctly pleased with it.

During the ensuing eight years, Tallulah scored several successes, including TV appearances, but she last appeared in 1967 on the *Johnny Carson Show*, and then retired into semi-seclusion.

She contracted flu, followed by pneumonia, and her fatal illness was in December 1968. Her funeral on December 14 was a tribute to one of the most superb actresses of the 20th Century.

MURDER BY MISTAKE

Variation on the time-weathered theme, "You can get away with murder before a Key West jury," proved valid again in the stabbing of Armando Andre Fernandez by his second wife, Betty L. Fernandez, on March 27, 1963.

The formula of drama seemed like the scenario for a dated movie: beautiful blonde woman, dark handsome man, an attractive other woman, a love triangle, and finally, in the French tradition, a "crime of passion."

Now for the prelude.

In the early 1950s Betty, the central character, was married and had two children. She was in her early twenties, vivacious and full of surplus energy. Some of this was channeled into participation in the Key West Players. In the summer of 1952 she appeared in a play named, ironically, *For Better or Worse*, among other theater offerings.

By 1954 Betty worked as a beautician for Alyce Milan, then Alyce Ryan, at the Casa Marina Beauty Shop.

Betty was good in her professional work, but was not approved of in regard to her treatment of another beauty shop technician, Gloria Fernandez. Gloria was the wife of Armando Fernandez, man-about-town, whom Betty had met and with whom she had become involved in a sizzling affair.

Said Alyce Milan, "Betty used to go to Donald's on Duval, the beauty shop where Gloria Fernandez worked, and have Gloria do her manicures. Then she would come back to my shop and laugh about getting beauty care from Armando's wife without Gloria Fernandez suspecting a thing.

It was reported that Armando and Betty became acquainted at a bowling alley and that bowling led in their mutual interests. In the courtship period with Armando, Betty lost custody of her two children by her first husband, when she was found negligent of child care by leaving the youngsters alone. She explained that this apparent neglect was due to an unreliable baby-sitter.

The father retained custody of the children when he and Betty had divorced. By 1959 Betty's name appeared in the city directory as Mrs. Armando Fernandez. They were wed in the middle 1950s.

All went bowlingly, as it were, for several years. Armando and

Betty had two children, but in about five years the marital state began to disintegrate. Armando had a roving eye and time to rove.

Acquaintances recall that he encountered a young woman from Cuba who worked at Hilda's Restaurant, in the vicinity of Margaret and Catherine Streets. Another heart intrigue shaped up. Caridad spoke no English, and she found Armando's appeal enhanced by his bilingual ability. She evidently had great charm and a warm Latin-fire quality, for Armando became enamored.

His wife, Betty, went to Washington, her home state, on a visit. When she returned, she learned that her spouse had developed a serious liaison with the Cuban girl, who was in her mid-twenties, some years younger than Betty, who was then 32. Armando was 34.

Halloween is a time for pranks, but the mischief-making that began the season in 1962 was not a joke. Mrs. Fernandez began getting telephone calls informing her that her husband was "cheating" on her. Earlier, in September, she got a call to inform her that Armando was visiting Caridad, who then lived on Petronia Street. Betty went to Caridad's dwelling, and found her husband there. He admitted that he had been "going" with Caridad, but swore they were finished. He asked Betty to be patient, to leave him alone and not ask questions.

All this cropped up in flashbacks during the subsequent trial when Betty was charged with killing her errant husband.

So Mrs. Fernandez attempted to comply with his request, doing housework, washing his clothes, cooking his meals, taking care of the children, and trying to achieve a level emotional attitude by taking tranquilizers. It was brought out that the drugs she took to calm her were followed by stimulating drugs, and that the ultimate reaction was a disturbed mental condition.

Then, driven to distraction by jealousy, she asked her husband to choose between herself and his mistress.

Armando's machismo asserted itself. He got an apartment for his mistress and himself, establishing at 1115 Margaret Street a "love nest," as they used to say in the 1920's scandal sheets.

By that time Betty was obsessed with getting Armando away from this other woman. She kept calling him, begging him to come back to her. He agreed to anything, at least on the surface, to get Betty to let up on the annoying pleadings. But the truce was only temporary. November of 1962 provided new evidence that Armando had strayed from the home fold again, but Betty could not accept the circumstances as they really were.

She learned that her husband had been frequenting Monroe

General Hospital, where Caridad was a patient. Once she waited in the car while he made a visit to his ill mistress. He paid the hospital bill and tried to convince his complaining wife that he was doing so in order to set Caridad on the path of recovery, and that when that happened, he could break off the relationship.

Betty even bought flowers to send the hospital and signed her name as well as Armando's to the card. Armando tore it up.

After Caridad was released from hospital care, Armando continued to pay her rent, buy groceries, and give her a weekly forty-five-dollar allowance. Raging with frustration, Betty followed her husband to a meeting with Caridad on Johnson Lane. Betty slapped Caridad, then remained for a three-way conclave. Around Thanksgiving of 1962, Armando insisted that they file a divorce petition. This was later withdrawn, and the embattled pair continued to live stormily together.

Christmas Eve, 1962, Betty drove their car (here is the scenario's touch again–it was a lavender Cadillac) to a party at a bowling lane. Armando had said he might show up later in the evening and that Betty should go ahead on her own.

At the bowling rendezvous, Betty met a male friend, and they decided to go to the Gold Coast Lounge in the lavender Caddy. The friend drove. Betty explained, "You always let the man drive." But Armando took exception to the incident. He seized all of Betty's jewelry from her except for one ring.

The New Year of 1963 rolled in. There was some improvement in the loosened marriage ties. Betty noted later that her husband took her to dinner three times. Then, as she observed during the trial, "Bang! The bottom fell out again." Matters between them became more tense. Armando began staying away from his home base for longer and longer intervals.

Betty's life was made more intolerable by telephone messages taunting her about her husband's infidelity. The climax exploded on the evening of March 27, 1963. A man phoned Betty to goad her with the information that Armando was at 1115 Margaret Street with his mistress. He turned on the power in the prodding, saying he was telling her what was going on because Armando had been messing around with his wife, too and, "I want to get even!"

Betty waited on the porch of her house in pajamas and a robe, expecting Armando to come by eventually. He finally drove up in a car with friends. When he stopped, Betty pleaded that she wanted to speak with him. He grew angry and ordered her to go inside, then drove off with his companions. Sure that he had gone to Caridad's place, Betty dressed and decided to go to the Margaret Street "hideaway."

Picking up the testimony at the subsequent trial, which was held the following January, the violence on March 27, 1963, unfolded with significance.

Betty told the court, "As I was going out the door, I picked up a knife (a twelve-inch letter opener) because I had to go through a bad district of the town, and I was afraid. I rode a bike to 1115 Margaret Street. I saw my husband's car parked in front of the house."

The apartment was dimly lit, and it was about 10 P.M. Betty could not see through the jalousied windows, but she heard Armando talking inside. She moved to the porch and listened to a conversation in Spanish. "I tried the door, but it was locked, so I knocked. I heard Caridad ask who was there and I replied 'Marina' because I knew that if I said 'Betty' she wouldn't have opened the door.

"But the door did open, and I saw her standing there behind my husband. She was wearing a negligee."

The newspaper account of the courtroom scene was described by Jim Cobb, reporter for the *Citizen,* in an admirably written story:

> At this point, Betty rose up on the witness stand and became hysterical. She said, 'I just wanted to get her. I tried, but my husband grabbed me. I didn't mean to hurt him. I loved him. He was trying to keep me from her. I heard him fall on the floor, and I saw he was hurt. I told him I would get him a doctor. There were people all around, and nobody would help me. Don't you understand? I didn't mean to hurt *him.* I don't remember anything further that happened that night.'

Another version, derived from piecing together connected events of that fatal night, was that Armando opened the door and Betty, thinking Caridad would have been the one to do so, lunged blindly and stuck her husband right in the heart with the weapon.

She also managed to slash Caridad's arm, but when she saw that her husband had fallen and was bleeding, she dropped the long blade and attempted to revive him. Caridad escaped, screaming, to a neighbor's. When police arrived, they found Betty crouched over Armando, attempting to bring him back to life.

She was taken to jail immediately. She awoke next morning and repeatedly asked about her husband, evidently unaware that he had bled to death at the scene of the attack.

106

Bond was first set at $25,000, and Betty remained behind bars for some time. Eventually, the amount was reduced to $5,000, and she was released under bond in April 1963. Her father came from Bremerton, Washington, to be with her.

Trial was scheduled for January 13, 1964, at the Monroe County Courthouse. The charge was second degree murder. Presiding at Criminal Court was Judge Thomas Caro. The prosecutor was Broward County Solicitor Thomas Coker, Jr. Attorney for the defense was Henry Carr of Miami. Associate defense counsel was Key West's own astute J.Y. Porter IV.

The opposing attorneys were known as "courtroom strategists."

The interpreter employed was Charles Parra of Key West. His services were invaluable, since the chief witness, Caridad, had such little knowledge of English.

The six-man jury had been fairly difficult to select, since so many who were called admitted prejudice in the case. The foreman was Charles Loudon. One juryman was Winthrop Biddle, a resident from Philadelphia who later became an eccentric Key West character. Another jury member was Thomas Harper of Sugarloaf Key who, in the aftermath procedures, felt he had to "justify" the verdict.

Betty Fernandez was applauded by the spectators when she appeared the first day, and sympathy, at least on the part of women at the trial, was openly expressed.

In the beginning, Caridad said she had had no personal contact with Mrs. Fernandez, but on the second day of the five-day trial she stated that once Betty had tried to beat her up and threatened to kill her.

Prosecutor Coker lashed out at Betty, accusing her of being a home-breaker. "Fernandez was a married man when you met him. You broke up that marriage," he proclaimed.

Betty replied, "I didn't consider that I broke up that marriage," inferring it was already "shot."

Coker then remarked, "When you returned from a trip to the Northwest you found Caridad doing to you what you had done to Gloria, Armando's first wife."

Stung, Betty retorted, "That was entirely different. I didn't torture anyone!"

Coker cut in sarcastically, "You just stole a woman's husband."

Seventeen witnesses were called, and the prosecution tried to bring out in cross examination that Mrs. Fernandez was not the loyal wife she was supposed to be. Her image as the devoted mate, although perhaps marred, remained intact for the most part.

The trial played to huge crowds in a five-day sequence. Defense counsel J. Y. Porter hammered away at an important impression based on sex. He said, "She was a wronged woman, driven to the point of desperation by an indifferent husband." Attorney Carr underscored that Mrs. Fernandez was "acting in defense of home and family."

Prosecution's main line of attack was, "She took it upon herself to act as judge, jury and executioner, instead of the divorce court procedure." Addressing the jury, Coker averred, "If you give a 'not guilty' verdict, you are saying she had the right to do as she did. The honor of Monroe County rests with you. Yours is the ultimate decision as to what kind of law enforcement you will have in your community."

What kind indeed?

On January 17, 1964, after five tumultuous days packed with excitement, the jury brought in a verdict of "not guilty."

The accused sobbed when the verdict was read. Then she threw herself into her father's arms, then turned to embrace her attorneys, Porter and Carr. She rushed to thank the jury, and there was a babble of tearful happiness.

Prosecutor Coker, according to reporter Cobb, "…appeared dumfounded by the verdict."

But all Key West was not in accord with the outcome. A bitter feeling against the widow was disclosed in arguments over the verdict. On January 20, arson was committed by two unidentified men who burned the $4,000 lavender Cadillac–property of the deceased Armando which Betty was still driving around town. She also received threatening telephone calls telling her to get out of town.

Since Mrs. Fernandez was considered not legally responsible for Armando's death because she had stabbed him accidentally instead of her intended victim, she could expect a widow's rights to her share of his estate. She was made official administratrix of her husband's property, since he had died intestate. The claim was filed January 28, 1964.

Two claims against the widow's right were filed by Armando's mother and his sister, but Betty objected. The relatives did not pursue litigation, and after three years their claims were dropped.

Final settlement did not come until August 21, 1970, when Betty left all heritage rights to the children, who had been six and four years old at the time of her trial. The final documents were signed by Betty in 1970, and her name had changed.

She had married again.

SOUTHERN EXPOSURE

Old streakers never die, they just run away. Out of sight. But not out of memory!

A few years ago the streaking craze, which meant stripping off clothing and racing naked through a community area, was popular all over the country. Key West was no exception.

A favorite track for the runners was South Beach to Louie's Back Yard, right along the shoreline. One bold streaker began to dash down Duval Street from the Bull and Whistle, but he kept ducking into doorways and only made it for a block.

The fad didn't last long on the island, probably because current beachwear fashion bordered on the point of no return anyway.

Perhaps the early fadeout of streaking here was simply due to its being dull and repetitious. Most Key Westers had already enjoyed forerunners–now there's a likely pun–of the streaker impulse on a much more complete and hilarious basis.

One episode which engaged attention involved the time when a U.S. Navy sailor was hauled into a hearing conducted by the late Justice of the Peace Ira Albury at his Duval Street "J.P." chambers adjacent to where Al and Ethel Brown now have an antique shop. Albury was a very tall, gaunt man with a somewhat sour expression. But he had a fine sense of humor and good insight into human behavior. Word had gotten around, and the room was jammed with curious townspeople.

Chief complainant was a young, recently married woman who had acquired the local nickname "Calamity Jane" because she was given to reciting woes of her existence before and after marriage. She loved to confide in friends and even in comparative strangers whom she met while working as a waitress.

I remember distinctly one of her "worrisome" recitations. It concerned her inability to chose a suitable mate from a series of suitors, mostly Navy men in the area. In a flat tone she revealed, while serving me a spaghetti dinner, "I have thirteen guys writing to me and proposing. I just don't know which one to accept." Whereupon she lamented having to make a choice. She finally decided, and married not one from the enlisted list, but a civilian.

At the hearing, the wife appeared anxious to disclose what had taken place, but it was only by astute questioning on the part of

Albury that what had transpired was revealed.

According to testimony drawn mostly through a question and answer technique, the victim was asleep on her side of a wide bed also occupied by her sound-asleep husband. Calamity Jane said that she was aroused from deep sleep by the feeling of strong arms about her and a nuzzling of kisses on her neck in amorous intent.

The woman admitted that she responded sluggishly and had not even opened her eyes during preliminary action.

Albury queried, "You mean you didn't wake up when the... ah, first moves were made?"

The witness shrugged and answered, "No, sir. This happens all the time with my husband, so I didn't pay it no mind, at first."

Albury lowered his glasses, looked over their rims at the woman on the stand, sighed, and shook his head while listeners exchanged glances. Albury asked, "What made you finally come to the conclusion that the man in your embrace was not your husband?"

After a significant pause, the wife raised her hands. In a widespread gesture, she measured off about two feet in span. Before she could explain in full, the spectators registered loud guffaws. Albury pounded his gavel and threatened to clear the court, but he himself engaged in a halfway grin.

Calamity Jane went on to explain the measurement maneuver. "I mean, I could tell this man wasn't my husband by the difference in the width of his shoulders."

She went on to tell that she then noticed her spouse was asleep beside her. So she screamed and poked him until he was aroused at last. He finally responded to the commotion and sat up. The stranger began stumbling out of the bedroom.

The husband was not wearing pajamas, but he didn't stop to don any garments. He took off after the retreating prowler, who was also unclothed. The two men ran out of the house, and the wife, in a nightgown, followed them screaming, "Stop him!"

Lights were switched on in the neighborhood and people emerged to witness the chase in bewilderment. Someone called the police and a squad car caught up with the disrobed men, who were then grappling on a lawn several blocks away.

It took some effort on the part of the law officers and everyone concerned to sort out the facts. Spectators couldn't quite grasp the reason why two stark naked men were racing around in an otherwise respectable community. The enraged husband was finally escorted back to his domicile, and there police discovered the orderly arrangement of discarded seaman's attire on the porch, along with the proper identity of the amorous prowler.

The eventual outcome was the sailor's arrest and transfer to some other city, but no discharge. In fact, it was suspected that the woman in the case had known the unfortunate sailor and that he was one of her former suitors.

The compulsive, or perhaps acquired, characteristic of military neatness, such as the careful placement of clothing after stripping for nocturnal adventure, had several repeated incidents that spring back in the early 1950s.

I was living in one of the downstairs apartments in a pink building on Charles Street with a watchdog named Claude M'Collie. Across the central hallway were two young girls, one employed by the Navy yard and the other a corn-fed, unsophisticated visitor from the Midwest. Upstairs, above the girls, were rooms occupied by a Navy couple, Lois and Larry Dimmick.

We were all aware of a string of incidents involving trespassers and Peeping Toms which had mushroomed on the island. As a result, the girls across the way had developed a signal between their abode and the Dimmicks's just above them. The Dimmicks were the only ones in the four-unit structure with a telephone.

Arrangements were made so that if a disturbance took place, the tenants downstairs were to take a broom or mop handle and pound on the ceiling in rapid succession to indicate distress. Lois was then to call the police and also notify the Shore Patrol, since at that time there was a conflict of duty on arrests.

I left my place, with Claude M'Collie on guard, and went up to cover a new show at the Overseas Lodge in the Keys, escorted by Commander and Mrs. Robert Zimmerman. Gladys Zimmerman, who wrote a column called "Shop Hopper" for the *Citizen*, recalls the evening vividly. She remembers that we returned shortly after midnight and, homeward bound, had discussed the rash of clothes-shedding episodes.

When we reached Charles Street and my dwelling, we were stopped by Shore Patrol officers and local police. We watched while a hunched-over captive, enveloped in a blanket, was hustled into a police van. I was questioned by law enforcement personnel and finally allowed to enter the apartment, there to be greeted by a frantic collie dog very upset with all the disturbance. The other inmates of the complex had been huddling on the porch. As soon as 'the law" departed I began questioning occupants to find out what had really happened.

It turned out that the visiting girl had returned from a date with a Navy friend at about 11 P.M., and stumbled over the neat pyramid of a Navy man's apparel on the front porch of the apartment. She said she simply glanced at the clothing and went on into the front crosswise hall connecting the two sections of the apartment.

There she encountered a naked man trying the door of my apartment, my dog barking protest.

As she told it, she gasped and turned left, frantically rapped on the door to her friend's apartment, and was immediately admitted. As she surged into her friend's room, she blurted, "There's a naked guy out in the hall!" The incautious roommate started to open the door to confirm this blast of information, but the panic-stricken guest slid the bolt on the door and exclaimed, "No, no! He's still out there somewhere!"

Meantime, the trespasser had blundered into a utility closet, staggering around upsetting buckets and mops, creating further racket. Then he climbed the stairs to the second floor and began trying doors again.

Mrs. Dimmick sat alone, hoping her husband could get off duty early, since it was her twenty-first birthday. She glanced at the door to the living room and saw it bulge inward a little. She arose and was about to open the door in anticipation of Larry's homecoming, when she heard the danger signal knocked on the ceiling below her. Immediately aware that there was trouble lurking outside, she dialed the police department, explained the situation, and then called the Shore Patrol.

The frightened inmates downstairs continued to send the prearranged S.O.S., and the interloper persistently pushed at the Dimmicks's door. That's where the rescuing forces discovered the intrusive, unclad visitor, still trying for admittance.

Later, when I interviewed the girl who had first encountered the nude visitor, I asked, "Why didn't you yell when you found him?"

She cast down her eyes, blushed, and replied, "Well, I was so embarrassed I thought I would just ignore him."

There were even a couple of women who joined this strange penchant for casting away garments during those past years, although neither of them was careful about folding up discarded garments.

On Thanksgiving Day a group of friends, including Leila Godfrey, Louis Strong, an artist, Viola Veidt, and myself, were invited to enjoy a turkey dinner at a home on Vernon Avenue. The host and hostess were comparative newcomers to Key West. The wife was a former entertainment world figure who knew a long list of songs from the 1920s and 1930s, especially, and she was a delight to hear.

We all trouped to the home in great anticipation of a double feast–food and fun. At first our knock on the door was unanswered. Then, as we were beginning to wonder if the 1 P.M. time had been changed, the house door was flung open and there stood our hostess, without a stitch of raiment.

"Come right on in," she invited, "and you can start cooking the turkey." She staggered, blew boozy kisses, and weaved her way back to bed. With the help of the host, who was also pretty far gone in Thanksgiving cheer, we managed to get dinner under way and enjoyed a holiday meal, although it was late evening before all the food was ready to be served.

The other skin flick appearance involving a woman considered a "socialite" from New England, who was a winter resident. She had been a model in her younger days and still thought of herself as a "femme fatale." A far-gone alcoholic, the ex-model carried a bag the size of an old-fashioned reticule, in which she concealed a quart of liquor, scotch or rum.

I was slightly reluctant to accept an invitation to bring a friend and come swimming at the Key Wester pool, where the ex-model had a cabana. But she seemed to be sincere and sober, so I went, accompanied by Helen Wirmusky, a school teacher anxious to enjoy an afternoon relaxing poolside.

After a couple of hours of sunning and swimming, we returned to the cabana. A water show was due for rehearsal that day, so we were in a rush to get dressed and watch some of it before leaving. Helen, the teacher, and I failed to notice that our hostess had left the cabana. Then the telephone rang. A male voice with a ring of authority asked for the hostess. It was then we discovered that she was missing. Since she had been clad only in a kimono-style dressing robe, I was sure that she was nearby.

"This is a guest of Miss (name omitted intentionally), and I think she is out along the pool," I said.

The voice on the wire stated coldly, "We are well aware of that. What we want you to do is get Miss ------- back into the cabana and see to it that she dresses and leaves the premises immediately."

Helen and I went outside, and there was our tall, thin hostess parading at the edge of the pool, grandly, with model's studied postures, but flinging her robe open to expose her body sans even a whisper of underwear.

The water show rehearsal was, of course, temporarily suspended.

Participants stood around giggling. Some spectators were aghast; others simply ogled and howled with laughter.

We managed to hustle Miss ------- into seclusion and get her attired by threatening to leave her stranded. The management called twice during this interval to hasten the exodus.

The exhibitionist hostess was the talk of the town for that season, and for several more to come–although today she might warrant just a lifted eyebrow.

PLAYBOY OF THE
KEY WESTERN WORLD

The late Harry Howard truly earned the title which I bestowed on him during the 1960 Key West winter season. Dubbed "The Playboy of the Key Western World," Harry lived up to his reputation with persistent vigor.

Harry was compactly built, not rugged, but with an athletic control of body movement, which indicates a tennis player, and the fluid coordination of a good swimmer. He had a squarely-contoured face, wore heavy, horn-rimmed glasses which concealed the exact color of his eyes, and flashed a warm smile. He projected an over-all Ivy League image.

I met him at one of the "round-the-island" parties which abounded and bounded in the late 1950s and early 1960s. At first glimpse I tagged him as an ultra-conservative businessman, inclined to be of the stuffed-shirt variety, of New England heritage. My initial impressions of Harry Howard were soon scuttled.

I've never been so off-target in a personality estimate, before or since! The only characteristic category in which I scored was in my opinion that Harry had a flint-hard and sharp business instinct in the Yankee trading tradition. His shrewd business mind lasered in on getting a Yankee dollar whenever, however he could, and skip all that benevolent Coca-Cola connection. Just make it straight Caribbean rum!

In the fitful Fifties, the pierced-ear craze for males had developed. There was some sort of code for men, who usually wore only one earring. Which ear was pierced and adorned indicated whether the wearer was homosexual, straight, or, as the slang term, AC-DC in sex habits.

Harry went along as "undeclared" in preference, but he certainly liked the ladies. So he decided not to wear ornamentation in his ear lobes or even in a nostril, as some people of the era–males and females–were doing.

"I prefer to have an unusual place for display of any decoration," he intoned. So, with the aid of a friendly surgeon, he had a convenient aperture bored in a private part of his anatomy. This provided a secure place for display of jewelry, or a cluster of flowers... a sort of boutonniere, although, of course, not anywhere near the lapel.

He usually picked hibiscus, for the big flamboyant blooms were not only spectacular and in keeping with his spirit of exhibitionism, but were easy to obtain. The tropical flowers grow in practically every yard in Key West.

Harry went in for flower show sprees only at the height of private parties and, except for these special occasions, was decorous in behavior. Also, he performed only at the behest of his hosts, unless the frenetic festivities went on at his own home. Everyone in the party-going set expected him to add to the madcap celebrations. Eventually his blossom caper no longer surprised the members of the regular merrymaking circles. But it jolted the uninitiated, and that was what provided Harry with his wacky "kicks," just watching the expressions on the faces of his audiences.

The Howards owned and operated a curio/gift shop in Nantucket in the summer season, and vacationed in Key West during the cold months. Harry said that one reason he loved it here was that he could do some real beachcombing along the Keys. He was always on the lookout for unusual items that could be sold as souvenirs in his New England gift outlet.

Early in 1960, the Elsa Maxwell/Perle Mesta male counterpart, Rex Brumgart, famed for his unusual party themes, dreamed up one on Tennessee Williams's drama *Suddenly Last Summer*, which had been made into a sensational movie. In it Katherine Hepburn was cast in the role of the haughty aunt who lived in New Orleans and kept a bizarre, exotic conservatory/garden filled with exotic plants, such as the Venus Fly Trap, which captures insects or even tiny animals, and consumes them at leisure. Instead of ferocious plants in a garden, Brumgart devised a stage setting for his parody play, using the mounted heads of game trophies of animals and some stuffed fish. The piece de resistance was the head of a lion severed from an ancient lion pelt rug. The head was placed on a draped box facing the audience, which was seated around the living room of the Truman Avenue house, where the crowd had gathered for fun and games and refreshments, including a powerhouse punch that put everyone in a receptive state of mind.

Harry was fascinated by the massive lion's head, its fierce, glaring glass eyes, and the open, snarling jaws exposing long fangs.

Playwright Williams himself attended the event and enjoyed the deviations on his dramatic creation. After the performance, Harry was persuaded to augment the entertainment in the fashion to which we had become accustomed–striking postures, posing and dancing, flourishing the posy arrangement. Suddenly, while twirling around the head of the lion, he stopped and shouted, "Where is the rest of it?"

"The rest of what?" demanded Brumgart.

"The rest of the lion", Harry yelled. "What did you do with it?"

"Well, the rug was moth-eaten and most of the fur was worn off right down to the hide, so I threw it out."

Harry grew more excited, asking, "Where? Where did you toss it? Quick. Tell me!"

He was informed that the rug-pelt had been discarded in a trash heap across the street in a parking lot where there were big trash cans.

In agitated haste, Harry began pulling on his trousers without removing the attached flowers. He just jammed them inside his pants, and the zipper stuck so that some of the hibiscus remained on the outside of the garment.

"I've got to have that rug," Harry exclaimed. "Just think of the claws I can get from the paws! Marvelous for necklaces or key rings. What items for our shop!"

He borrowed a butcher knife from the kitchen and a pair of pliers from a toolbox. He stuffed them into the pockets of his trousers, a brand new pair in patchwork quilt design and an array of assorted colors, the very latest fashion in resort wear for men. He didn't bother to pull on his shirt. But he did think to scrounge a flashlight from his host, and then dashed out the front door and ran across the avenue to the almost-deserted parking lot.

The lights there had been turned off an hour before. It was then one o'clock in the morning, but the flash had a powerful beam, and Harry soon located his coveted prize. He couldn't wait to take it back to the house to examine it. He yanked the pelt out and spread it on the lot's concrete surface. Sure enough, the paws on the rug were intact, and Harry was elated.

However, people who lived in adjacent houses were alarmed. All they could see was the naked torso of the man crouched behind a disposal container, flicking on the flashlight and brandishing a long-bladed knife. The steel could be seen gleaming in the rays of the flashlight. The figure was partially concealed in shrubbery near the trash cans, but this didn't interfere with the sound effects that accompanied glimpses of a thrusting knife. The madman was singing a number from a Gilbert and Sullivan light opera, according to the frightened but music-minded woman who telephoned to the police.

The patrolman arrived, sans siren in order to sneak up on the prowler. He drew his nightstick, but not his gun, and crept silently into the parking reserve where he could see a bent-over, shadowy figure intently working with a knife on something lying on the ground... something that looked like a bundle of rags... although it could be a... The officer extracted his own big flash and pointed the glaring stream of light on the mysterious crouched bushwhacker.

The ensuing dialogue occurred between the hunter of souvenirs and the bewildered hunter of a suspected wrongdoer, perhaps an insane murderer:

Cop: "What are you doing there?"

Harry: "I am pulling the lion's claws. Oh, good evening, officer."

Cop: "Lay off distractions. I asked you what you were doing in the bushes."

Harry: "And I told you the truth. I was pulling the lion's claws."

Cop: "What lion? And you come out in the open with your hands up! But bring all the weapons with you.

Harry: "Okay, but I don't want to let go of my lion."

Cop: "You got it on a leash?"

Harry: "I can explain everything, sir. Just give me a chance."

Cop: "Okay, but come out of there. Put your hands above your head and bring all that stuff with you."

Harry stood up, clutched the precious lion's pelt in one hand along with the pliers. In the other he held the borrowed butcher knife and the flashlight. He staggered out into the open lot, and the cop looked at him with astonishment.

Cop: "Drop everything at your feet and brace your hands on the car hood."

Harry obeyed and was frisked for concealed weapons. As the policeman encountered the protruding flowers in the region of Harry's trouser fly, he froze and backed off to have a more thorough look at Harry's getup.

Cop (with a snort of disgust): "What the hell is this?" Then he examined Harry's crazy quilt pants. "What kind of costume is this? You were at a masquerade party?"

Harry: "Well, no, it wasn't exactly a masquerade. It was a *Suddenly Last Summer* party."

Cop: "I thought you said the party was tonight, not last summer .Just where is this party?"

Harry: "It *is* tonight. It's just across the avenue and probably still going on. We called the affair *Suddenly Last Summer* after a Tennessee Williams play."

Cop: "Hmm. Well, that accounts for a lot of these weird goings-on, I suppose."

At this point the exasperated police officer kicked at the pile of discarded rug/pelt. Harry protested.

Harry: "Please, sir! Don't disturb that pelt. You see, that's what I've been getting the claws from and I want all of them."

Cop: "Let's see your I.D. and driver's license. Who are you, anyway?"

Harry: "I sell whales' teeth and I am a beachcomber."

Cop: "You sell whales' teeth? I thought whales were an endangered species. Where in hell can you sell their teeth? Besides, we don't need beachcombers in Key West. I think I oughta run you in at least on suspicion."

Harry: "Look, sir. I'm not just a beachcomber *bum*. I am a beachcomber *professional*. I search beaches to pick up curios and gift items for my shop in Nantucket. I thought that since whales' teeth were a best-selling item–I just find them on the shoreline, I don't kill whales for their teeth–I thought that lion's claws would be a similar souvenir to sell at my place. The pelt rug was given to me so that I could extract the claws."

The patrolman sighed. He finally realized that Harry might be a nut, but he was a harmless one, and the cop had had a busy day. Besides, the jail was already overflowing. So he said, "Well, I'll let you go this time. But don't let me find you trying to pull any more lions' claws or twist lions' tails. Now pick up your belongings and get the hell out of here!"

Harry alertly followed the command and prepared to walk back across Truman. The policeman pursed his lips as he once more surveyed Harry's ensemble, the flower clump in front, and then noted one last oddment! From Harry's belt hung the lion's tail, which he had chopped off from the rug and thrust into his belt. There it swung as Harry sauntered off, trying to appear nonchalant and singing to himself.

The cop had one more question. "What's that first line of that tune you're singing?" Harry decided to be bold. "It begins: '0! A policeman's lot is not a happy one . .'"

The officer nodded in agreement. "You can sing that again, brother!"

STREET PEOPLE:
CALEDONIA AND CRAZY HELEN

Caledonia is the poetic term for Scotland. It is also a street in London where a fabulous flea market is located. And it is the title of a foot-stomping tune from several decades ago. The song's opening phrase was, "Caledonia, Caledonia! What makes your big head so hard?"

But to old-timers in Key West, Caledonia is the name associated with one of the town's most startling and literally colorful characters. I never learned her full name in the past, and query even now has been unsuccessful. I suspect that some of the people questioned knew the real name, but refrained from revealing it out of consideration for relatives. So, just "Caledonia" will suffice for this word sketch.

Caledonia was of medium height, but looked taller because of her style of dress and high heels. Hats piled with millinery frippery, which Caledonia often wore over afro pig-tails, contributed to the illusion of tallness.

Caledonia was considered one of the better seamstresses in Key West's Black community. She fancied herself a dress designer, and she created individual ensembles of clothing for herself. Rumor had it that she did well in this field until suffering the trauma of a blighted love affair and developing a "disturbed personality."

She frequented the Aronovitz dry goods store in the 600 block of Duval, carrying a paper sack containing pennies and small change. She would rummage around, selecting remnants of cloth, ribbon and lace.

Bernie Dickson, the jewelry store owner, who not only recalls Caledonia herself, but also talked to sales clerks, said that tourists at nearby Ramonin's Restaurant would leave their tables, rush out and snap photos of Caledonia in her bizarre getups, which could be regarded as a forerunner of some of today's styles.

The first time I saw Caledonia she was wearing one of her monochrome ensembles in yellow, but she also favored other pastels: pink, blue, green, lavender, and rose. Her ruffled and flounced gowns were accompanied by accessories in matching color. Gloves, shoes, hats, and handbag, with perhaps just a shade of tone difference depending on the material, composed the symphony of tints.

To top it all, she flourished a frilly parasol in the chosen color.

Pirouetting and dancing, Caledonia loved to admire her reflection in the windows of stores up and down the main stem. She preened herself in the mirrored front of the Aronovitz emporium especially. She liked to dance on the street corners and collected tossed coins.

But she wasn't always ladylike, to say the least. The florist and manager of Southernmost Flowers and Gifts, 616 Duval Street, was Johnny Knight. He says she used to stand out in front early in the morning yelling, "Who's gonna buy my breakfast?" and begin cursing unless placated with at least a quarter.

Jeweler Paul Sher recollects that every merchant in the area met her money demands just to get her to leave the store premises. "She pestered everybody."

When she swaggered into bars demanding money, she was often greeted with the loud and lusty rendition of the song "Caledonia" but with alterations, substituting the word "fat" for "hard" and changing the word "head" to "rump." Well, that's the polite version.

However, there was one occasion when Caledonia overstayed her visit to a bar and was forcibly ejected by the proprietor. She promptly reentered, bent over, flipped up the back of her skirt and answered the ditty singers with a yowled, "See for yourselves."

Toward the end of her bouts of capricious behavior, which grew rowdier and more profane, even her style of dressing changed. She seemed to be making a parody of her former careful color blends, and appeared in a cowboy hat, a bright red blouse with Cuban-style ruffled sleeves, and a Seminole Indian skirt with multi-hued bands encircling it. The final touch of "originality" was a pair of bright blue, fluffy-feathered boudoir slippers.

I prefer to remember Caledonia as contributing to the legends of Key West. I personally saw one incident which proved she had a genuine sense of humor.

A smart haberdashery was operated in a frame building across from La Concha Hotel on Duval Street. It was known as Stinchfield's, after the owner, George Stinchfield, also fondly called "Stinky." He had a quality shop in Palm Beach and was well informed on the latest gadgets for displaying resort wear for men. Chic mannequins of wire and basketweave straw, with simple body outline, were imported. The dummies were wigless and had oval shaped heads; the faces were featureless.

One day, fascinated, I watched Stinchfield dressing his window with the mannequins. Then along came Caledonia, prancing in lavender finery. She paused, peered at the window setup with a perplexed expression at first. Then she splayed hands on hips, rocked back on her heels and laughed hysterically.

She shrieked, "Just look at them dummy things. Ain't got faces! And people say that I am the crazy one around here!"

Other street characters drew attention. One dowdy woman called "Crazy Helen" roamed the streets with a beat-up baby carriage crammed with empty beer cans. If she encountered another

woman pushing a baby buggy, she would ram it and declare, "Look at my baby. Just as pretty as yours." One summer Crazy Helen acquired a moth-eaten raccoon coat, and in the heat of August she wore it, parading proudly along the pavement, and, like Caledonia, admiring her reflected image in the store windows.

That coat had a rich subsequent history. Roy Passwater, who was arrested once for urinating in public behind the police station, inherited it. Roy, who died a few years ago, used to wait for me at the door of Carlos Food Market on Caroline and Elizabeth, which was across the street from the cement porch where the winos used to hang out. Roy would hold the door open for me as I left, sweeping his coat in a grand gesture reminiscent of Sir Walter Raleigh.

The late artist, Bruce Mitchell, claimed Helen must have had a stage career some time in her past, although she never disclosed anything of it. He cited a happening to prove his point. Helen used to hang out around Fisherman's Cafe, the old yellow building on Caroline Street which had long been a favorite subject of artists re-creating local scenes. It was moved to Whitehead and Front, next to the Conch Train Depot, in 1981.

One day Bruce was sketching the cafe, and he noticed Crazy Helen, who had a mobile face coarsened by age and cheap wine, but with a certain strength to it. He asked her if she would pose for him.

Helen considered a few seconds and then said, "You will have to wait until I get my makeup on straight." She had no compact or comb or any facial cosmetics at all, but she had imagination, for she retired coyly behind a telephone pole and went through all the gestures of applying makeup, after setting up an imaginary mirror.

She kept peeking around at Mitchell while she daintily applied foundation cream, then went ahead patting on rouge, powders, eye shadow, eyebrow pencil, and lipstick in precise professional detail From time to time she fluttered her eyelashes and asked, "How do I look now?"

Finally, slanting a rakish hat over her forehead, she consented to sit for her portrait sketch, maintaining a somewhat arrogant posture. When Bruce had finished several preliminary sketches, Crazy Helen demanded to see results. With a grande dame attitude, she examined the work and remarked, "I can't say you have done me justice."

The grapevine tingle on Caroline Street reported that Helen, last name unrevealed, had finally been hospitalized and died of "complications."

TENNESSEE WILLIAMS

Playwright Tennessee Williams celebrated his 70th birthday by opening a new play March 26, 1981, at the Goodman Theatre in Chicago. It was a comedy called *The House Built Not To Stand.*

Williams rules as a leading figure in writing not only plays, but also short stories and poetry, and is an artist of national acclaim.

I first met him in a more personal way than a casual "Hello" in passing, or at a party. It was some time in the 1950-51 period when he was in Key West with his grandfather, the Rev. Walter Edwin Dakin. Viola Veidt, who assisted me at the Southernmost Flowers and Gifts Shop, at 616 Duval, knew Williams well, and invited him and his grandfather and Frank Merlo, Tennessee's companion, to dinner at the apartment downstairs in back of my shop. Viola was known as an excellent cook, and the invitation was accepted with pleasure, much to my excitement and delight.

The Rev. Dakin was fondly referred to as "The Bishop" by most people who knew him. He held a Doctor of Divinity degree but was not a high church official, although he was a beloved minister of the Episcopalian faith.

I surmise that his title of "Bishop" was applied because of his dignified, courtly demeanor and his expression of serene wisdom. He was distinguished in appearance with almost handsome, well-defined features and an erect bearing. He seemed stern at first glance but, although he wore very heavy-lensed glasses and was slowly going blind, there was a discernible twinkle in his old eyes. He was also nearly totally deaf. He smiled readily and maintained a soothing, benign expression and manner.

I had a singular bond of rapport with Dr. Dakin, since I, too, had a severe loss of hearing in both ears. I wore a powerful hearing aid and was able to hold down a newspaper job despite the handicap. The deafness began when I was twenty-one years old, a senior in college, but the reduction in ability to hear was so gradual that the extent of damage to my inner ear bone construction was not diagnosed until I was thirty. By that time, the atrophy of the auditory nerves in both ears was beyond repair. The original deterioration of the tiny middle ear bones was due to concussions from horseback riding accidents and retention of water in the interior ear passages from swimming and diving while in my teens.

Tennessee was concerned and curious as to why, at my age (in my early forties), I was as hard of hearing as his grandfather, who was half a century older.

He asked, "Are you *sure* that your deafness isn't psychological? You know it is possible that you have had a psychological trouble which makes you want to shut out the ugly sounds of the world and take refuge in loss of hearing."

He admitted there were occasions when he wished he could will himself to do just that, adding, "Especially when I am concentrating on some difficult phase in writing."

That evening of the dinner, we had cocktails in the small downstairs living room, and "The Bishop" accepted a small glass of wine and beamed on the intimate gathering. He couldn't hear any of the general conversation, but he would respond if a speaker raised the voice level to almost a shout and projected the words directly into his ear.

After Viola's more than "satisfactory supper," Tennessee persuaded his grandfather to try out the spare hearing aid which I kept in case of mechanical failure of the one in use.

The test was not a success, as I predicted before the attempt. To have correct sound conduction, the ear mold attached to the aid must fit snugly in the ear canal, as near airtight as it can be. Otherwise, "feedback" will produce squeals and whistles that are both distracting and painful, since the insertion of the aid plug ends close to the eardrum. Since every mold has an individual form, mine would not adjust to the Rev. Dakin's ear canal, and we had to make do with a loose-fitting commercial ear plug. The ensuing experiment was disastrous. All that confusing sound, due to the poor connection, made the old man extremely uncomfortable and self-conscious. He would only catch occasional snatches of conversations. Finally, he slyly turned the switch off altogether. I couldn't blame him, although Frankie kept urging him to persist. "You'll get used to wearing an aid if you keep trying," he said.

Dr. Dakin continued to smile and nod as if he were adjusting. It was a supreme gesture worthy of a stage performance, but he was just being polite. When Frankie used a couple of cuss words, and "The Bishop" still continued to be approving, it was a give-away to the turned-off evasion tactic he employed. Finally, the "try-on" was also turned off. The Rev. Dakin sipped his wine in comfort, and his expression of contentment wasn't faked. I don't think he ever got around to acquiring a hearing aid. He lived until he was ninety-eight and had lost his sight, although he never complained of his plight.

The topic was dropped for the rest of that evening at my house, but Tennessee remembered this incident. I realized years later that he had taken it all seriously, with due consideration and attention.

I concealed my hearing aid and my disability, in part, by wearing a spray of either real or artificial flowers over the ear in which the aid plug was inserted. Williams used this fact for an illustration in one of his plays about women who suffered traumas, either physically, or psychologically, or both.

About ten years after that supper incident, Williams took part in a special mission to rescue me from my advancing hearing problem. I had learned that a surgical solution might improve my ability to hear more clearly. I discussed this in detail with writer James Leo Herlihy, who was also "simpatico," and who had become a close friend. So it was that in 1960 I made inquiry as to a potential inner ear operation which might restore at least partial hearing. But both the examination and the actual surgery would cost an amount far above my means as a staff reporter on the *Key West Citizen*.

Herlihy approached Williams with the idea of financing a journey to Florida's west coast for an examination of me by ear specialist Dr. J. Brown Farrior. Williams complied instantly, and he and Danny Stirrup–at the time his good friend–combined forces. I was given $600 for the expedition and was promised more if an ear operation was advisable.

Dr. Farrior completed the examination, but did not think surgery would help me. He advised me to keep informed, and suggested that, in time, perhaps only a few years, there would be a new type of ear surgery which might alleviate the ear condition, in part, and increase hearing range. I returned the money not spent for the trip and the examination.

It was not until 1966 that such surgery potential became a reality. By the time, I had group insurance at the *Citizen* and was able to finance my own operation costs.

I have been grateful through the years for the initial role Tennessee, Jamie Herlihy and Danny Stirrup played in helping me. This was just one of the playwright's unsung, unknown efforts to help others. I was only one of many persons who were given both financial and psychological boosts by playwright Williams through the decades and on into the present time.

Now back to my first encounters of acquaintance with Tennessee Williams.

One Christmas I was standing outside the Episcopal Church, at

126

the corner of Duval and Eaton Streets, watching crowds of worship-pers and gazers like myself, as they went to the special services. I was enraptured by the sound of the church bells, the chimes sounding out Christmas carols and hymns played in the church tower overhead. I sat on the church's Duval Street wall to listen.

Along came Tennessee Williams and Frank Merlo escorting and guiding the frail Rev. Dakin, now in his nineties and almost blind. Tennessee stopped and said, "I think I'll sit out here, too. It's such a lovely night." He sat beside me on the wall. "There is such a huge crowd, and I don't want to take up space needed by the regular church-goers."

So the Rev. Dakin, after shaking hands, tottered off with Frank Merlo tenderly supporting him. The two men entered the church.

Tennessee took out his customary cigarette, attached it to a long holder and smoked calmly. He was silent. I was sentient enough to realize that he was savoring the mood of that Christmas Eve, so I, too, remained silent. The perfume of incense wafted out of the church, and the music of the bells was replaced by the mellow deep tones of organ music played indoors to accompany the celestial voices of the choir.

After the special ceremony ended, Dr. Dakin came out again under the solicitous care of Merlo. "The Bishop" had a positively saintly cast on his gentle old face, and Frankie was beaming. We exchanged holiday greetings and said good-night. I think Tennessee was anxious to leave before being overwhelmed by the throng.

I developed a tremendous admiration for him as a friend, as well as for his writing, and I felt his brilliance and greatness as a writer cancelled any adverse criticism as to his personal behavior, and any gossip about him or Frank. I knew Merlo to be not only protective of Tennessee but a contributor to Tennessee's happiness.

In fact, during one conversation with Williams, he said, "I suppose people wonder why there is such rapport between me and Frankie. He is a balance factor. I'm a moody person. Frankie directs a shaft of light into the sometimes dark and gloomy spaces of my life. He's a spark for the fire of life for me." So when I discovered that two reporters, one of them a *Citizen* staff member, were plotting an exposé story on Williams and his relationship with Merlo for the scandal magazine *Confidential*, I called Tennessee and warned him of the machinations against him and his companion.

I told him to beware of a car parked near the house on Duncan Street, with one or more "investigators" in it, and that the vigil was being kept nightly, hoping to catch sailors entering the residence. One of the "snoops" was, in fact, a Navy man, and the other an ex-Marine. They both had approached me with the idea of my signing an affidavit which they could turn over to the magazine, in which I would aver that I had actual knowledge of and was a witness to the playwright being an avowed homosexual.

Remember that back in those days, three decades ago, this term was a condemnation, not just a label. The Navy man offered to cut me in on whatever sum they were paid by the scandal magazine.

Indignantly, I refused. I immediately informed my friend Williams of the undercover plot which was being planned in order to discredit him. All for the price of a byline in the notorious *Confidential!* (About 1969, *Confidential* was run out of business, having sustained countless lawsuits.)

Tennessee thanked me for the tipoff. I decided to find out more about the sneak attack. During this period I was still in communication with the schemers. One of them met me at the Gallery Lounge, corner of Caroline Street and Duval, where the Bull & Whistle is now located. We were sitting at the far side of the bar near a door that opened onto Caroline Street, sipping beer, when Tennessee came in with Frank Merlo and sat down at a nearby table.

I was apprehensive for a few moments, but Tennessee and Frank gave no sign of anything being amiss, and I exchanged greetings with them. Then Frank motioned me over to the table to join him and Tennessee. "Bring your friend, too," he invited, not giving any indication that he knew the reporter or that he was engaged in nefarious mischief against Williams.

There was no dodging the invitation. Besides, my newspaper colleague accepted the bid with alacrity. I felt uneasy, but followed his lead, and we moved to the table. Tennessee asked what we would prefer to drink. My "partner" stuck to beer, but I switched to rum and Coke, feeling I needed something stronger to boost my spirits, literally. After the drinks were placed before us, my colleague took a long pull at his suds and leaned back in contentment, completely relaxed. And that was when the ambush began.

Tennessee leaned across the table. With softly uttered subtle menace he said, "Now that you have accepted my hospitality, suh, let me ask you a pertinent question. I think I have earned the right to do so. Isn't it true that you are involved in trying to place me in a compromising situation? And isn't it true…" There was a dramatic pause, and then Williams's voice raised to a loud, firm pitch. "…that you are attempting to accuse me of admitting to being a homosexual?"

My colleague unfolded to his height of over six feet and backed up. "I don't have to answer you," he muttered. At that point little Frankie drew himself up to *his* five feet, four inches or thereabouts, and positively bellowed, "You son of a bitch! How dare you try to injure the greatest living playwright in the world!"

The owner-operator of the Gallery Lounge came to our corner, on the double, and made motions attempting to pacify the antagonists into silence.

Frankie remained belligerently cursing and very bellicose. Everyone in the Gallery Lounge was listening attentively. The proprietor joined the shouting match, yelling at the pianist, "Play, for God's sake, play! Play as loud as you can. Play as if you were on a sinking ship and there was panic."

The pianist complied. He pounded the baby grand and rendered "Nearer My God To Thee" in tones calculated to drown out all the cussing and exchanging of remarks on a then-taboo subject.

The humor of the situation got to me and I was convulsed with laughter. My erstwhile escort left hurriedly. The piano player continued to present the ship-sinking theme, and presently Tennessee began chuckling. It took a little more time for Merlo to calm down. But he, too, at last burst into laughter.

From that day forward, there was a real bond of rapport between Tennessee and myself, even when, at parties, there were hordes of distinguished guests in addition to Tennessee himself. I remained in awe of his brilliance and was always overwhelmed by his wit and keen conversational exchange. He always gave me a hug and an affectionate kiss whenever we encountered each other.

I left Key West for vacation the summer of 1953, and didn't return until the spring of 1955, so I wasn't here for the 1954 filming of *The Rose Tattoo* or for ensuing interviews. I freelanced in New York City, and did a stint with International News Service. When INS combined with United Press, and United Press International was formed by the coalition, I had to seek other employment.

In the fall of 1954, I left New York for a post as woman's page editor and columnist for the *Star-News* in Wilmington, North Carolina. I stayed with that newspaper until the spring of 1955. Then the publisher died, the paper changed hands, and the new publisher brought in his own staff. There were twenty-two members of the *Star-News* writing staff left stranded with only two weeks notice. What a scramble for jobs. I spotted an ad in the national *Publisher's Weekly* wanting a society editor for the *Key West Citizen*. I was already homesick for Key West and decided my best bet would be to return to my old stomping grounds. I sent a telegram to Norman Artman, publisher of the *Citizen*, and got an immediate offer to come back to the paper, plus a raise.

I arrived on the island in mid-April 1955, just in time to get re-established in the writing groove. The spring of 1955 was to be one of the most stimulating periods of my Key West years–in fact of my whole life, at least as far as writing goes–and it went at a gallop back then. In the later part of April, Tennessee Williams telephoned the *Key West Citizen* and asked if I would like to interview novelist Carson McCullers. She was visiting Key West, having a reunion here with Williams after a nine-year interlude.

A date and time was arranged for the interview, but Tennessee talked to me privately and personally before the actual session. He explained that Carson had gone through an extremely trying period: the suicide of her husband, Reeves McCullers; emotional disturbance; and a problem with alcoholism. All of that was followed by a stroke which had partially paralyzed her.

"She needs a morale boost," he confided. "She is working on her writing, but she feels depressed. I think a sympathetic and appreciative feature story might help her."

I had just finished an interview with Françoise Sagan, then a young French novelist and Tennessee's newest "protege." Sagan had come to Key West expressly to meet Carson McCullers. But that is another story. The playwright said that he had decided that I would be just the writer to treat McCullers with exactly the right mixture of understanding and compassion.

Somewhat overwhelmed, I rushed off to the library to reread *A Member of the Wedding*, which McCullers had written, and also *Reflections in a Golden Eye,* as well as *The Ballad of the Sad Cafe,* which was new to me. Thus forewarned about the recent past of the sensitive writer, equipped with knowledge of her best-known creations, I went to Williams's home on Duncan Street well-prepared, or so I thought. I was not ready for the impact of the actual meeting and the "inner force" projected by the frail-looking woman who had been Williams's close friend since 1946.

Virginia Spencer Carr revealed details of this long and tender friendship, or relationship, rather, since it was so profound, in her biography of McCullers, *The Heart Is a Lonely Hunter.*

Lula Carson Smith (the writer's original name) became Carson when she was sixteen. She dropped the first name at fifteen when she was in high school in Columbus, Georgia, in 1933.

Photographs and paintings of Carson reveal the vulnerability most evident in her mouth and her large eyes. In these pictures she appears to be a waif type, although some photo studies give her a more sophisticated aura. And all of the portraits, either by brush or by camera, yield the impression of a sensitive personality, whether laughing, pensive or melancholy.

On April 29, 1955, the day of my interview, I met McCullers with a great deal of timidity on my part and a subdued, retiring attitude on hers. Tennessee was the monitor in our person-to-person session, and he, of course, was exceptionally gentle and considerate with Carson. This attitude underscores Tennessee's thoughtfulness in helping others, for he, himself, had just endured an emotional upset. His beloved grandfather, the Rev. Walter Dakin, had died on Valentine's Day, February 14, 1955, after a stroke. He was two months short of being ninety-eight, and, of course, the death was to be expected. Nevertheless, the feeling of grief was acute. Yet Tennessee devoted his time and attention to Carson McCullers and her problems and interests.

After introductions in the living room of the Williams home, Carson sat beside Tennessee and posed for a photograph by Don Pinder of the *Citizen* staff. Her luminous, large, hazel-brown eyes looked directly at the camera, but she was unsmiling. She had magnolia-pale skin and a magnolia tone of voice, soft and somewhat elusive to me. I tried adjusting my hearing aid to her low decibel range, but there were several instances in which Tennessee had to repeat her answers for me. He was infinitely patient.

Mrs. McCullers's left arm was supported in a sling, and I later learned that she was enduring nearly constant pain. But she, too, was understanding about my handicap and extremely cooperative with my note-taking.

Like Tennessee, she declared that she found mornings the best time for creative thought. Said she, "I feel more inspired in the early part of the day." She was happy to be recovered enough to be writing again, and declared she was "proud to be part of the Southern Revival." She was referring to the surge of literature by a number of writers in the South at that period. She had adapted her own play version for *A Member of the Wedding,* and expressed gratitude to Tennessee for his advice and guidance. As she spoke of this, the rapport between the two friends was vividly apparent.

She admitted that she had written poetry, but had not submitted it for publication. In producing fiction, she did not make an outline because, as she explained, "The mood creates the story and then carries itself as I write."

As she talked, the writer ran her right hand through her tousled, spiked, brown hair, which was cut in a boyish cap-like style, adding to her French gamine appearance. In fact, she came of French and Irish descent and exhibited some of the gaiety of such heritage, as well as a trace of a moody quality, with a hint of a volatile and stormy temperament. But the predominant note during the discussion of her work was of gentleness, graciousness and an undercur-

132

rent of sadness. All of these traits were touched with a personal warmth and radiance.

Williams was certainly cognizant of this quality. In the section "Some Words Before," which appears in the introduction to Virginia Carr's biography of McCullers, he wrote: "Carson's heart was often lonely and it was a tireless hunter for those to whom she could offer it, but it was a heart that was graced with light that eclipsed its shadow."

Carson McCullers went on writing in various creative forms including scripts, stories and magazine articles, despite her growing ill health. Tennessee Williams continued his encouragement and friendship. In August of 1967, she had another stroke. She died September 29, 1967.

Carson McCullers had returned from Key West to her house in Nyack, New York, just before the exciting news arrived that Tennessee Williams had won his second Pulitzer Prize, this for his drama, *Cat on a Hot Tin Roof,* a dazzling success on Broadway that year. The award availed me of one of the most important assignments I have had in my thirty-plus-year writing career. I was sent by the *Key West Citizen* to interview Williams on the occasion of the Pulitzer Prize.

I was tense and nervous when arrangements were made to talk to Williams. I was aware that my story would be carried by the Associated Press, as well as by the *Citizen.* To me this was like a shot of adrenaline. Williams had been notified of his triumph by Music Corporation of America about 4 P.M., Monday, May 2, 1955. The AP call came through asking for a personal interview. Over the telephone, Williams agreed to a conference with me at 5 P.M., Tuesday, May 3.

Tennessee made an immediate effort to set me at ease, sensing my nervousness about the auspicious meeting. Grinning happily, he received photographer Don Pinder and me while reading batches of congratulatory telegrams. He was relaxed on a sofa in his living room, dressed casually in a blue sports shirt, dark blue Levi's, and brown loafers. He was sockless foot-wise, but not verbally. His conversation carried plenty of "sock."

He quipped, "I am waiting for a ham dinner to be prepared. Don't you think ham is apropos with theatre?" He chuckled at his joke.

His answer to my first question–which was standard: "How do you feel about winning the Pulitzer Prize this time?"–was frankly put.

"I got more kick out of this prize than the first one for Streetcar, because this time it was unexpected." He continued, "The play, Cat, as I call it, had a message dealing with the mystery of one person's relationship to another, regardless of intimacies. The applied interpretation is simply that two people can live together without really knowing anything about each other."

He was pleased that there had been no censorship angle so far. He commented, "Even in Philadelphia, no old ladies came to the box office to complain. There was only one change in the original script. A Southern slang word was put out–the term 'humping' was eliminated."

He declared, "The stage has more freedom than movies or TV shows." He also expressed agreement with Director Eli Kazan in the selection of the cast. Barbara Bel Geddes played the original part as Maggie. (This triumph was repeated in 1974 with Elizabeth Ashley in the leading role. The movie version placed Elizabeth Taylor as the heroine, and Paul Newman was cast as the reluctant husband.)

The New York Drama Critics' Award also went to Williams in 1955 for *Cat on a Hot Tin Roof.*

Tennessee has been sympathetic toward women consistently, not only in his plays but in real life. At one point in the late 1950's he aided and comforted Diana Barrymore, helping her to overcome acute alcoholism and to attempt a comeback in her acting career. She wanted to marry him, and her affection for him was genuine. But the rehabilitation effort wasn't successful. She died in January 1960 of a heart attack, after taking too many sleeping pills. It was never determined whether this tragedy was an accident or suicide.

I recall one incident when the playwright's patience with the female sex gave way to exasperation, but it was more humorous than serious in consequence. Williams was in the throes of creation and required solitude. One day he returned home after a beach excursion to find the little Duncan Street house buzzing with the chatter of a group of club women. He had forgotten that they had been invited to view the home and grounds. In a furious verbal attack, Tennessee ordered all the ladies off the property, shouting in no uncertain terms.

There was momentary confusion and an aftermath of criticism, but not by any of the more discerning local women who had intelligent insight into the angst of genius, and he was forgiven. A great many club members even accepted the situation with a shrug and laughter at the spectacle.

On the credit side of the ledger, I was witness to his hospitality and kindness when a bustling bevy of women travel writers converged on the island, and a tour of the Williams residence and grounds was on the entertainment agenda.

The date was January 17, 1971. The late Mary Louise (Mrs. Ray) Manning of St. Louis was hostess, and she joined with the playwright, his Boston terrier Gigi, and a cat called Gentleman Caller in greeting top fashion and travel writers from commercial publications in the United States and France. Tennessee even acted as interpreter for a visiting French editor, with skill and courteous, warm graciousness.

When Tallulah Bankhead was in Key West as a guest of author James Leo Herlihy, Tennessee made it a point to attend the weekend sessions held at the night spot All That Jazz, when the incomparable Miss Bankhead appeared to sing throaty versions of ballads. Despite their differences of opinion on some stage matters, he wanted to help Tallulah in her effort to add to her theatre triumphs. He gave her a "pep talk boost" on her rehabilitation obstacle course.

Nineteen years after the 1955 Pulitzer Prize award, Tennessee was given the annual Award of the Association of St. Louis West Libraries for outstanding contribution to literature. The event took place at the Pius XII Memorial Library, in St. Louis, Missouri.

Tennessee was suffering from an attack of the flu and said so in a brief accepting speech. He quipped, "I have not been able to prepare a long speech, and some may consider this an act of God."

Ray Manning, a St. Louis public relations man, and then husband of Mary Louise Manning, who had become Tennessee's close friend, wrote to me describing the ceremony for my *Key West Citizen* column, "Conch Chowder."

"As to the award presentation, the newspapers do not signify anything as to how skillfully Tennessee played to the audience of more than 1,000 in strictly ad lib and very glib fashion. He has really become a fine performer. His audience caught little intimate glimpses of him as a person, as well as a playwright.

"Later, seated beside him prior to dinner in his honor, I observed him fielding inane questions and signing numerous autographs.

"Then a man approached and said, 'Mr. Williams, I have

never been able to find a character in any of your plays who resembles your brother, Dakin. Did you deliberately omit him or is it that he is just too normal to have been included?"

Ray Manning reported further, "Tennessee leaned back, folded his arms and announced to all present, 'I have talked with many people; I have answered many questions; I have signed many autographs. I have made an accepting speech–and now I feel that I have earned the $1,000 that I get for this appearance... And I am not going to answer another question or sign any more autographs.' So saying, he worked through the crowd and left."

I retired from the Key West *Citizen* in 1977 to join the staff of the monthly Key West newspaper *Solares Hill*. I interviewed Tennessee Williams on May 11, 1981, for my *Solares Hill* column, "Notes and Antic-Dotes."

The appointment for the interview was made for 1 P.M., to take place at Williams's home on Duncan Street. JoAnne Savio, the *Solares Hill* photographer, was assigned by editor/publisher Bill Huckel to take pictures and to transport me to the interview. JoAnne arrived in time to pick me up at my house on Peacon Lane, but with no spare time margin in case Murphy's Law intervened. Murphy's Law dictates, "If anything can go wrong, it will." And it did!

Since I don't drive, I am not familiar with side streets not in my immediate neighborhood. Nor am I acquainted with street changes and the lack of signs of direction. I knew that Duncan Street turns off White Street, but not exactly where. And somehow we missed the street. Before I was aware of having passed the turn to the left, we were wandering around in the boondocks.

To complicate matters, the streets were being dug up for sewer installation, and some of the street markers were missing. I grew more perturbed as we searched, since I am a stickler for promptness on assignments, and I was in a "dither" when we finally drew up at Williams's house.

I was nervous and aflutter with apology for being tardy, even though not much off schedule. However, the welcoming committee, headed by Tennessee himself, who met us at the front entrance to the cottage nestled in its tropical setting, was evidently forgiving, and Williams was at his most gracious. He was accompanied by a large, deep fawn-colored purebred English bulldog with a friendly canine grin on its white-blazed face. Immediately inside the living room, we were introduced to Frank Anton Krause, the capable and courteous secretary with whom I had talked via telephone, and auburn-haired Terry Daniels, a young man exhibiting a pleasant smile.

Tennessee was garbed in a muted tropical print shirt-and-shorts set. He looked handsome and fit, flashing a good-humored smile. His well-groomed beard and mustache are still darkish but touched with gray, as is his casually-brushed hair. He wore tinted glasses, but the discerning look he gave us held a twinkle.

We were gestured through the front room toward the outdoor living-room patio which is a step down from the dining area next to the modern kitchen. And there I shook hands with Leoncia McGee, long-time faithful retainer-housekeeper, whom I had not seen in years. Just the sight of her face reminded me of past years of happy encounters, and I relaxed.

We sat around a large round table with a cracked marble top, at ease in rattan chairs placed with inviting casualness about the table.

The bulldog came waddling up for attention, wriggling and wagging his screwcut tail. I asked his name.

Tennessee said, "It's Cornelius."

I quipped, "Vanderbilt, no doubt." And I got a quizzical glance from Tennessee. It was only later, when I was back home contemplating the afternoon session with the great playwright, that I recalled "Cornelius" was also Tennessee Williams' father's name. It also turned out to be the name of the central male character in Tennessee's recent play, *A House Not Meant To Stand*. There is, undoubtedly, a psychological implication in the name of Cornelius being applied to the dog, but I choose to let that pass.

While JoAnne unobtrusively took photographs from all angles, Tennessee and I got down to direct facts about his drama, *A House Not Meant To Stand*, which would premiere at the Goodman Studio Theatre in Chicago on March 26, 1981, Tennessee's seventieth birthday.

"It's a gothic comedy," he explained, "humorous in some aspects, but also tragic and a little bit bizarre." He made this last remark with a small quirk to his mouth, and after I had read some of the reviews I decided he had made an understatement, deliberately.

"The time is contemporary and the setting is in Pascagoula, Mississippi, on what is known as the Gulf Coast," he noted.

He dismissed for the nonce my question as to detailed story line, saying, "The theme is much too complicated to state in a few words. Besides, the play is still in the third revision and this has not yet been submitted to the Goodman Theatre. It is being rewritten under the same title, *A House Not Meant To Stand*, but the original was called *Some Problems For The Moose Lodge*, a one-act creation."

Continuing, Tennessee said, "I will tell you that this revision requires a female star. Maureen Stapleton would be ideal." Tennessee knows her quality and ability from the past. She has appeared, and re-appeared, in several of his most successful offerings and the replays. In 1951, Stapleton undertook the difficult role of Serafina delle Rose in *The Rose Tattoo*. Another Tennessee Williams' production in which she acted was *Orpheus Descending* in 1958. She also received plaudits for her interpretation of Amanda Wingfield in the May 1965 revival of *The Glass Menagerie*. She kept repeating the roles, and by 1975 was thoroughly established as Tennessee's favorite star. She was selected, too, for screen versions of Williams's *The Fugitive Kind* and *Twenty Seven Wagons of Cotton.*

Time, on May 18, 1981, less than a week after my conversation with Tennessee, stated, "Stapleton pilfers top acting honors in the Lillian Hellman drama, *The Little Foxes.* The review conceded that Liz Taylor was dazzling, but that Maureen Stapleton, as Birdie, the genteel alcoholic, was "not tearjerking, but heart-rending."

Tennessee admits that he is a "compulsive writer." Even when he travels he writes and re-writes. His working schedule is the same as it was when he was younger. "I still get up at the crack of dawn, sometimes at 4 A.M., and write before eating."

After lunch, or brunch, he paints. At present, he is working on a portrait of the late playwright, Eugene O'Neill. He alternates this with portrait studies of his mother, Edwina Dakin Williams, who died not long ago when she was in her nineties.

He works with acrylics, and had a large easel set up adjacent to the marble-topped patio table. It is surrounded with tubes of paint, jars of water, palette knives and other art accessories. He declares he prefers portraiture to landscapes or still life paintings.

Williams has completed several portraits of his mother, but he tends to try for perfection in art, as well as in his writing, and keeps returning to a subject for modification, improvement, or a new perspective and conception. There is one medium-sized portrait of "Miss Edwina" beautifully framed, on display in the dining space. She is seated, or rather, enthroned, with a graceful pose in a wicker garden chair, and her charm is captured with tender poignancy. Even in old age, she was a beautiful woman.

While the playwright was delineating his painting sideline, and how a session at the easel was followed by swimming in the afternoon in the pool, in wandered Monsieur Topaz (pronounced with proper French accent). He is a large, longhaired Persian cat of a tawny, light-sherry shade. He leaped onto the table. After stretching, he ensconced himself like a noble feline monarch, lying down to survey us and now and then submit to the fond caresses of his master. Topaz's leisurely attitude, although he is somewhat rumpled as to grooming, was somehow apropos of the "laid-back" atmosphere of Key West.

The immediate future for Williams included a trip to England in the coming summer. Then late in the summer season, he would be in Vancouver, British Columbia. In fact Gary Tucker and Tennessee Williams planned to "open shop" in Chicago, working together. The journey to Vancouver was theatre-motivated. Said Tennessee with a contented smile, "I'm doing a very free adaptation of Chekov's *The Sea Gull.*"

This endeavor was actually a culmination of a deep appreciation of Anton Chekov. In the foreward to his *Memoirs*, Tennessee mentions a promise once made years ago, "to do a new adaptation of *The Sea Gull* and of a yearning to direct it." He remarked that he had fallen in love with the writing of Chekov and his short stories as far back as 1934, when he first read the Russian's work. Williams says he is "still in love with the delicate poetry of Chekov's writing." He vows that Chekov was, and is, the greatest influence on his own writing over all the ensuing years.

Asked if the many changes in Key West, especially during recent years, had altered his opinion of the island, he answered that despite violence which had brushed his life here, his attitude had not changed much. He still regards his Key West residence as a good place to work and to relax for intervals. As one newspaper story expressed it, "He is not a man of retreat."

The fact that Williams brought his beloved sister Rose here to live in this community is a positive indication of his basic fondness for The Old Rock, whatever troubles have surfaced here.

It had been announced that Williams promised to write a new play for the New World Festival, to take place in Miami in June 1982. Queried on this, Tennessee shrugged and commented, "At this early time I'm not even going to think about it!"

Director Gary Tucker, who was then in Key West, came by to talk with me and brought a number of revealing reviews of Tennessee Williams's recent plays, including *A House Not Meant To Stand.*

There were other articles on the playwright. One, by Helen C. Smith, expounds on his personality, stating "Tennessee Williams is a charming rogue."

He looks at least a decade and a half younger than his actual age and expresses himself with wit and modern phraseology, such as "I'm hanging in there, baby."

In my conversation with him on May 11, I recall commenting, "In a photograph of you as a very small boy, you looked like a blond, curly-headed cherub. But you turned out to be an intriguing devil!" He arched a grizzled eyebrow and chuckled in acknowledgement.

Both Williams and Tucker believe that a less ordinary formula than that of comedies and musicals should be introduced more often at all theatres, including local ones. The lack of fresh, more flexible programs hampers improved and expanded development in the art of the theatre.

Tucker, who directed Tennessee's *The Frosted Glass Coffin*, as well as *The House Not Meant to Stand*, would like to direct the very latest of Tennessee's plays in Key West.

The name of the prospective play is *And Now the Cats With Jeweled Claws*. The action takes place in the coffee shop of a downtown department store and features two older woman, a maitre d', and two male hustlers. Tucker says the play is "way out." It incorporates music and dance and Williams's later style of "fragmented" dialogue.

So much more could be written about the genius of Tennessee Williams, it would take an entire book to blanket the subject. I can only write, in conclusion, that I remain a devoted and fervent admirer of a great playwright and a great, compassionate human being who consistently contributes to the ever-changing field of writing, with his brilliance and, above all, his consummate understanding of life.

ONLY IN KEY WEST

"Conch Chowder" was the column I wrote for the *Key West Citizen* for approximately twenty-five years. It was so named because a little bit of every subject matter that you can imagine went into the makeup of column material. I picked up the idea from an old ditty, *Who Threw The Overalls In Mrs. Murphy's Chowder?*

As "Conch Chowder" became more popular, I expanded it, and as it grew longer and more varied, I introduced subheads to divide topics of presentation. One of these was "Only in Key West." It derived from a catch-phrase, a sort of *Catch 22* label, which applied to all the odd, hilarious, strange, startling and sometimes ribald happenings which I found in existence on the island. Some of the happenings were due to personal experience and contact; some were brought to my attention by contributing readers and companion "Chowder Marchers," a number of fans who liked to participate in recording happenings in my column. The incidents invited amazement and laughter and much shaking of heads and murmurs of, "Only in Key West could this occur."

In 1949, during the early period of my venture into Islandorama drama, the most repeated source of chuckles bounced from a mattress factory on Front Street, where the Florida First National Bank parking lot is situated. The mattress manufacturing concern had a sign in its window that said, "Marriages Performed." The proprietor was a notary public.

Around the corner and two blocks up Duval Street, a restaurant-bar prospered. It was the original Key West Delmonico's, a popular gathering place for local VIPs. It was not a gay bar then, but had special entertainment. The Saturday Night Special was loaded–with an act starring a trapeze artist named "Alma." She was a tiny woman who perched on a swing which wasn't very high above the heads of customers. She was advertised as the only trapeze stripper in show business. She did a few acrobatic turn-ups and aerial somersaults like "skin the cat" maneuvers, and swayed back and forth over the bar crowds as she discarded her costume, except for a couple of strategically placed chest tassels and a glittering G-string.

Alma remained as a stellar attraction until she grew jealous over attentions her boss and lover paid to a woman patron. Then she erupted into a positive dynamic fury and, leaping from her trapeze, destroyed the bar area, smashing glasses and bottles, ripping out bar service equipment, and attacking the bar habitués. Police came on a riot call, and she was finally ejected from the premises and hauled off to the hoosegow.

The trapeze hung suspended from the ceiling long after Alma had swung out of the picture.

For years, the back room of the establishment was the rendezvous of city and county politicos and officials. The walls of the special dining room were painted with a jungle motif mural depicting a troop of cavorting monkeys. The simians had monkey torsos, but the faces were caricature portraits of all the prominent men about town, with emphasis on members of the legal profession, especially judges.

Another favorite after-dusk assembly point was Duffy's Tavern, also on Duval Street, a few doors north of the entrance to Charles Street where Don's Green Room, a pool parlor frequented by neighborhood players and hordes of Navy personnel, was located. So much for all that furor over protection of sacred portals of Old Town historical sites and "protection of Duval from becoming a so-called slum!" Protesters against street vendors should have been here and seen the same section back then!

Duffy's Tavern was a combination barroom-restaurant and night club. A tremendous bar took up most of the space, and there were trophy heads of all kinds of animals including moose, certainly not native to Florida, studding the walls at intervals.

The show was a mixture of singers, dancers, comedians, who might be called "stand-up" except that they could hardly remain upright, victims of the occupational hazard of exposure to liquor.

The band, directed by Jerry Pinder, was very good, with Gould Curry at the piano and some excellent local talent on drums, sax and trumpet.

Duffy's was included as a stop on a Honky Tonk Tour operated by Cmdr. Harry Fitch, retired naval officer, and a retired naval chief, Dutch Schultz. They had a Volkswagen which took visitors to museums, historical points and a general daytime survey of the island under the label "Cultural Tours." The lettering on the sides of the bus covered both aspects.

One unforgettable evening, the dual-purpose tour bus, loaded with a throng of carefree sightseers who had been picked up at various motels about the island, stopped at Duffy's Tavern to permit the passengers to see the tavern's entertainment. After the performance had ended, the tourists filed outside ready to board the bus and go to the next stage of the nocturnal excursion.

142

Suddenly there was a sound of police sirens, and two police vans and three patrol cars came howling down Duval. The lead driver spotted the crowd of people waiting to re-enter the tour bus and mistook Duffy's for the night spot to which they had been summoned, a more rowdy bar just a block away. The police drew up with a flourish, and the cops surrounded the crowd of innocent, bewildered people in front of Duffy's entrance.

It took some frantic explaining before "the law" roared off to the right location on the mission in answer to a riot call.

One irate woman in the group of stunned tour riders stared at the lettered proclamation on the side of the bus touting "Cultural Tours." She shrieked, "My Gawd! So this is *Culture?*"

The late Nina Gulev was society editor for the *Key West Citizen* when I first joined the news staff as swing-shift reporter. I covered police and city hall beats at the old Greene Street edifice, conveniently across the street from the newspaper, and also the Navy, the county courthouse, the USO and the Chamber of Commerce. All on foot! I started out at 8 A.M. and was back at my desk by 11 A.M. to meet the deadline of 1 P.M.

I had to write my own heads for copy, but Nina left this task to Bill Lee, reporter and haphazard city editor. Lee was the source of a memorable headline on the society page: "BRIDE-ELECT FETED BY PRE-NATAL PARTY." This three decker was explained by Bill later. He had meant to write "PRE-NUPTIAL" not "PRE-NATAL." But he had been over to Sloppy Joe's, known as "The Citizen Annex," and was slightly slipshod in his thinking.

Bill wasn't always at fault for some of the more astonishing headlines. I caught a banner on a story which read, "Shrimper Breaks Leg in Wench." I corrected it to read "Winch," but to no avail. Someone in the "decomposing room," as it was dubbed, re-wrote the correct word "winch" and changed it back to the original "wench." Turned out that the self-appointed proof-reader was addicted to the Conch pronunciation and euphonic spelling. That also was the reason why a garden club story told how to care for "rack" roses instead of rock roses.

Perhaps the most hilarious of all misprints turned up in the third paragraph of a story written by Susan B. Anthony, then known as Susan MacAvoy, who wrote copiously for the *Citizen* about the scandal of Baer's Meat Market. The store sold horse meat under false pretenses advertising the product as being pure beef.

In the third paragraph or so after the lead of the report, there was a phrase that put readers in hysterics and the publisher in shock.

The story referred to a city ordinance and stated in bold terms, "Peddling of whores meat on the streets of Key West is forbidden." All but a few copies of that issue were recalled, but a few treasured, verboten copes were released. These became gems in collections of printing "howlers."

There was an optimistic note struck on tourism several years ago when large cruise ships, chiefly of Norwegian origin, stopped in Key West at least once a week on Bahama-Caribbean cruises. Passengers explored the "quaint" streets and browsed in shops.

During one such venture into the wilderness of wild and wooly Key West, a group of ship's passengers descended upon City Hall to rescue a couple of friends who had been charged with a minor offense, now forgotten. They mulled around in the lobby of the police department on Angela Street, awaiting the release of their chums. The incident had something to do with a slight argument with a native of Key West.

About the same time, a disgruntled townsman decided to vent his anger at having had a couple of his bubbas arrested and jailed in an unrelated incident. He drove by City Hall seething with resentment, and fired a revolver in the general direction of the lobby. Three or four bullets came whizzing in and were imbedded in the walls. Nobody was hit, but the unexpected upshot of events terrorized the huddle of cruise ship visitors. The matter with the jailed friends was peacefully settled and no animosity was expressed after all was clarified. They were escorted back to the cruise ship with apologies, but the general impression was that Key West was a southern-western frontier outpost and that vengeful shoot-outs weren't always staged in a corral.

Literally the "piece de resistance" of episodes was the French Connection, in the early 1960s. A flotilla of four French destroyers came into port, and hundreds of crewmen were given shore leave. On the first evening of the French Navy's "invasion," the streets, especially the main drag with its bars, shops, an arcade, and eating places, became the mecca of Frenchmen wearing summer uniforms and round, white, tam-shaped caps with red pompoms on the crown.

These pompoms became frazzled as the hours wore on, because the tradition, it was explained, was to remove a souvenir tuft from the red topknot and present it with a gallant gesture to any girl who permitted a kiss from a French sailor.

Incidentally, the romantic-acting sailors didn't just aim at young and comely female targets. Any age would do, as long as the female was willing. And plenty were! And so they thronged from watering spot to watering spot up and down Duval and its side streets, drinking and beating heart-throb drums until curfew at 4 A.M.

Despite this harmonious and hearts-entwined atmosphere, the *Citizen* reporter (Kay Kersey was on the beat temporarily that morning) visited the Old City Hall on Greene Street, and returned to the city room obviously shocked. She explained, "There are about a hundred French guys over at City Hall being taken to municipal court. Every one of them is charged with indecent exposure."

I burst out laughing and asked to cover the court story. I guessed in advance the cause of such mass charges. Around midnight before the fateful morning, I had seen a mob of the French navy men three and four deep around the tile basin and fountain in front of Luigi's, located where Dedek's Fogarty House outdoor patio is now. Curious, I took time from my nightclub route to investigate.

The sailors were taking turns using the fountain for French relief.

City Court Judge Enrique Esquinaldo raised an eyebrow and his gavel, along with his voice, as he called the court to order. The babble-gabble of mingled Spanish, French, and English phrases simmered down momentarily, but kept rising in heated waves along with Gallic and Cuban explosive phrases and dramatic gestures. Police officers, American and French naval officers, and some irate property owners, thronged the courtroom seats, and there was standing room only.

Judge Esquinaldo heard all the accusations and protests with great aplomb. He sorted out the explanations which spouted from all concerned.

The explanations were not watered down, although, in a manner of speaking, that was the original complaint. The accused declared that the City of Key West was not hospitable or civilized, as they did not provide necessities of living, such as corner pissoires, as was done in France. So what was a distressed sailor to do in the last analysis but use brushes, trees and walls, which offered poor concealment?

One scathing remark by English-speaking French officers in defense of the misdemeanor of the destroyer crews on shore leave was, "Key West is primitive, indeed, barbarous, in not providing accessible sanitary facilities for the public."

And certainly the palms newly placed in big pots in front of stores in mid-town provided no privacy at all. After the deluge, the calm; even a shining ray of international sunshine.

The lengthy discussion left everybody bushed, in a different connotation, of course. Judge Esquinaldo smiled with an impish expression and pronounced that, in the name of international good will, all charges against the French visitors were dismissed. He added in a quirkish mood, "I only hope that the potted palms on Duval Street will survive."

And so townspeople bid adieu (pronounced with a wink–"Ah, dew", and we give you French leave!

There was one aftermath that somewhat dampened the buoyant feelings. Somebody sent my punning, lightly-meant column to French naval authorities. I received an admonishing letter in serious answer to my humorous approach. One marked passage in the reprimand pointed out that, while distressing, the harmless and obviously necessary misbehavior on the part of the Gallic sailors, was nothing compared to what France, especially Paris, endured from American military men abroad.

In defense of Key West let us note that at least a few local outdoor privies were decorative, or rather, decorated with murals. The endeavor was done by an aging semi-vagrant with a flowing beard, who kept dropping into the *Citizen* to try to get Don Pinder, chief photographer, to come take pictures of his "masterpieces."

"Old World Charm," the name by which we knew him, painted the doors and exterior walls of outdoor toilets which ran to average size three-seaters, but sometimes were expansive five-seaters. He featured palms and sunsets and banana trees.

In contemplation of the constantly changing parade of town characters, I must acknowledge "Cigarette Willie." He was always a loner, and I never heard him speak. He crouched with a comfort blanket and a paper sack or two, usually on a street bench under the banyan tree that canopies the corner of Simonton and Eaton streets near the Old Stone First Methodist Church. Cigarette Willie always dangled an unlighted cigarette from his mouth, hence his nickname. He wore cast-off garb which was apparently exchanged for clean outfits once a month.

I never saw the color of his eyes, because he kept them closed, dozing, or seeming to, by day and sleeping on the bench at night.

Yet one bank official said that Cigarette Willie came to a local bank to collect a monthly stipend by which he lived adequately, eating fast food and sipping soft drinks.

The rumor was that his mental torpor and state of withdrawal came from a tragedy which sent him into permanent shock, a fire that killed his wife and two children and his destroyed home. That's why he never touched a light to the cigarette that drooped from his

146

lips.

After a final winter of discontent, or least of detachment in his solitary world, Cigarette Willie faded from the local scene. Presumably relatives had taken him away to a mental hospital, but that, too, is only surmise. Quien sabe? After he left Key West, he was sighted in Hawaii.

Derelicts and winos held little companionable share-togethers on the street side porch of the Old Carpenter's Hall, corner of Elizabeth and Caroline Street, every afternoon. There they drank Thunderbird wine and sometimes passed around a rare pint of hard liquor.

One of the group was a slightly built man with snow-white hair and aristocratic features named Roy Passwater. He had courtly manners, for instance, opening the Carlos Market doors for neighborhood girls and women. He accompanied this gesture with old-fashioned bows and offers to carry grocery bags for ladies.

Yet for all his polite manners, Passwater lived up to his name. He was once arrested for urinating in public at the Greyhound Bus Station, adjacent to the police station on Angela Street. He died recently, a charity patient in a local hospital.

A retired businessman I know says quirkish happenings have always been part of the pattern of life on "The Old Rock," as far back as he could remember, even in his boyhood. To illustrate the point, he said that his mother had come under severe criticism from the PTA when he was attending grade school at what is now known as junior high school level.

When in his teens, he sold magazine subscriptions around town, and one of the best sources for sales was at a house of ill-repute. His mother was not aware that the house was on the list of her son's customers. Nor was she aware that her husband, who was a wholesale beer distributor, also delivered the bottled beverage to the same bawdy house. She was a devoted mother and wife concentrating on her household duties and had no interest in anything to do with business aspects.

But the young boy, and also his father, were observed entering and departing from the premises of the notorious location. These sightings were reported to members of the respectable PTA, who in turn repeated the observations to the fellow members of the group. The lady was told that her spouse *and* offspring were seen at a den of iniquity. The distressed woman was horrified, although of course the suspected culprits were only on innocent missions.

I don't know how the father solved his problem; after all, the beer he sold was bought in great profitable quantities, and the depression was on here. But the lad who sold the magazines had to drop that particular location on his route.

Ironically the best selling subscription at the bordello was *The Literary Digest*, a now-defunct publication favored by intelligentsia.

Now for a look at the Key West city ordinance enforced in most of the shops, restaurants, and public buildings, and certainly by the more staid business institutions, such as banks.

There are notices in windows and on doors of these enterprises advising, "Shirts and Shoes Required." Most sign readers get the message clearly, and recognize that persons are asked to wear proper body covering and footgear. But the British interpretation is that a request is being made, as at a collection site for the underprivileged. For despite trendy fashion and antisocial behavior as far as youth riots are involved, average people from the United Kingdom don't even think of appearing in public streets without at least a semblance of appropriate clothing.

The same ordinance promoted a genuine "Only in Key West" incident observed and reported by Gloria Bollens, who was operating a Greene Street imported-items shop, "The Hand of Man." Gloria liked to eat a robust breakfast at Pepe's Cafe, the relocated one now on Caroline Street. She was savoring a third cup of Cuban coffee at the counter, when she heard an alien sound, a rustling, crackling, swishing noise. She swerved round on her counter stool and beheld two street loiterers (that's a polite term) shuffling into the restaurant, feet and legs encased in big, brown-paper grocery bags.

One of the breakfasters pointed to the city ordinance sign and croaked, "We gotta obey regulations, lady. And Carlos Market helped us out for covering our feet."

The final phase connected with the enforced ordinance cropped up during the Christmas season of 1979. The hour was within five minutes of the deadline closing time for Florida First National Bank. The guard was screening would-be entrants to the bank when a frantic young man pushed open the entrance door, waving a fistful of money. He was evidently trying to deposit it before the 2 P.M. shut-out. He got inside the sacred portals, but no further. He was halted by the guard just over the threshold, who indicated his shirtless state and barred his way.

The young man-in-a-hurry was garbed only in swimming trunks. He bolted out to a parked car and got a man to loan the shirt right off his back.

Back the barriers. But no avail. This time the uniformed watchman pointed to the second no-no: bare feet.

There were only two minutes left before the 2 P.M. closure of the bank. Distraught, the rejected man stood on the pavement, again thwarted and dejected.

Suddenly he had an inspiration and held hurried consultation with a Salvation Army representative, another youthful man, who was in charge of a big collection kettle on the sidewalk. The kettle man snatched off his shoes and handed them to the guy in distress. Never was a Salvation Army rescue act more appreciated.

The nervous would-be customer slipped into the borrowed brogans and made it safely inside the bank right in the nick of time. Even the guard laughed and spectators applauded. I'm sure contributions dropped into the kettle were rewardingly increased by the giving gesture of the Salvation Army guy, who stood there in stocking feet on one of the coldest days Florida had experienced that winter of 1979.

The concluding chortle for "Only in Key West" is contributed by Richard Marsh, editor of the 1981 edition of *Key West Collection*. He noted that officials in Key West keep a wary eye on travellers with meager visible means of affluence, and who are likely prospects for becoming panhandlers who often bother legitimate tourists. So a prominent City Hall representative, observing passengers debark from a Greyhound bus one day, watched with interest as three "hippie types" got off the bus. One disheveled fellow knelt down, kissed the gritty cement, and murmured, "Thank God, I'm in the Promised Land at last."

"Excuse me," said the official, touching one of the ground-kisser's companions on the shoulder, "Could you tell me what your friend meant by 'The Promised Land?'"

"Yeah, man. We got run out of Atlanta, Georgia," explained the "dirtbag," as they are branded here. "We went to Jacksonville, Florida. When we got the bum's rush there, we tried West Palm Beach, then Fort Lauderdale and finally, Miami. The cop who ran us out of Miami gave us advice. 'Why don't you just go to Key West? I promise you, you can get away with anything there.'

"And so here we are, man, in The Promised Land."

The City Hall official added, "They didn't stay here long, either."